Claudia

Growing Up Yanqui

Growing Up Yanqui

RACHEL COWAN

THE VIKING PRESS   NEW YORK

FIRST EDITION

Copyright © 1975 by Rachel Cowan
All rights reserved
First published in 1975 by The Viking Press, Inc.
625 Madison Avenue, New York, N. Y. 10022
Published simultaneously in Canada by
The Macmillan Company of Canada Limited
Printed in U.S.A.

1 2 3 4 5 79 78 77 76 75

Library of Congress Cataloging in Publication Data. Cowan, Rachel. Growing up Yanqui. Bibliography: p.   Summary: The author recounts her life as a Peace Corps volunteer in Ecuador, and other related experiences, describing how she changed from being a naive believer in United States foreign policy to a critic of it. 1. United States. Peace Corps.—Ecuador—Personal narratives. 2. Cowan, Rachel. 3. Cuba—Description and travel—1951–   [1. United States. Peace Corps.—Ecuador. 2. United States—Foreign relations—Latin America. 3. Latin America—Foreign relations—United States] I. Title.
HC60.5.C695   309.2'235'0924 [B]   75–16334
ISBN 0–670–35597–6

Excerpt from *The Children of Sánchez* by Oscar Lewis reprinted by permission of Random House, Inc. Copyright © 1961 by Oscar Lewis.

Extracts from *The United States and Latin America* by Richard J. Walton, copyright © 1972 by the author, reprinted by permission of the publisher, The Seabury Press, Inc., New York.

To Paul, Lisa, and Mamu
and
Lourdes, Paula, Evangelina, and Lucía

ACKNOWLEDGMENTS

My gratitude to—

Paul, who gave each draft the constructive criticism it required and me the encouragement I needed.

Connie Brown, my perceptive sister, whose comments helped me to say what I meant.

George Nicholson, who trusted I'd finish; Susan Schwartz, who worked so thoroughly and enthusiastically with me; and Olga Litowinsky, who so calmly and thoughtfully pulled the book and me together.

The teachers and parents of the Purple Circle Day Care Center, who made such a good school that I could work secure in the knowledge that Lisa and Mamu were safe and happy.

Contents

Introduction

The cafeteria of the National University in Bogotá was crowded at lunchtime. My husband Paul and I were the only North Americans in the huge room. When Paul left the table to get a Coke, the scattered rustling conversations that had filled the air died down. For a second the room was quiet. Then hundreds of voices joined together in one swelling chant. "*Yanqui Go Home!*" "¡*Afuera Cuerpo de Paz!*" "Peace Corps Get Out!" Then "¡*Abajo el imperialismo yanqui!*" A student raised his arm to heave a bottle.

Paul walked slowly back toward me. We sat at the table, scarcely able to breathe, until the chanting subsided. My knees were wobbling, my stomach a knot. Quickly then, we slipped out the nearest exit, and our friends hurried after us. Fortunately, the angry students went back to their lunchtime conversations and didn't follow us.

Claudia, a young Colombian social worker who had been our hostess for the past week, hugged me. "Don't take those chants personally, please! They aren't yelling at you. They're angry at the Yanquis, and they're taking it out on you two gringos. I know that you agree with many of their ideas, but they don't realize that. If you two weren't my friends, I'd have been banging my tray too."

The reaction hurt more because Colombian students had invited us to eat in their cafeteria. We were on a field trip with a group of students from Guayaquil, Ecuador, where we had been Peace Corps volunteers for the previous eighteen months. Together with an Ecuadorian social worker, Paul and I were teaching a class on community development and had arranged for the students to come to Bogotá. We thought they could develop new ideas for work in their own city after seeing some of Colombia's more sophisticated social programs. Colombia is more industrialized, more populous, and slightly more progressive than Ecuador. Nevertheless, the people of Bogotá and the people of Guayaquil live under fairly similar conditions. Crowded in small shanties, they lack steady jobs, good schools, enough to eat, and medical care. Only a minority live in large comfortable homes with servants. It is this wealthy elite that holds the political and economic power, that formulates the government's policies.

The shouting in the cafeteria hurt us and frightened us, but it did not surprise us. Living in Ecuador, we had learned why those students were so angry. In October 1967, after eighteen months of exposure to and confrontation with U.S. diplomats and businessmen in Guayaquil, we were angry too. Their aid programs were ineffective. Their contempt for Ecuadorians shocked us at first, then disgusted us. I wished I could have shouted back at those students, "We're different! We don't like the way our government treats Latin America either! We're here to help!"

But there was no way we could have communicated with that angry crowd. The barrier of suspicion was too great. It had taken months of working, talking, and relaxing with people in Guaya-quil for us to break through their stereotypes of the gringos and to become friends. Some never trusted us. It took us long months, too, to free ourselves from our cultural values in order to open ourselves to Ecuadorian culture enough to see people as indi-viduals rather than as "victims of poverty."

Underlying Latin American anger is the widening economic chasm between the United States and the countries of Latin America. Like the gap between rich and poor in Ecuador, it grows each year. While the economy of the United States ex-pands, millions of people in Latin America have less to feed their families than they did the year before. Each year there are more hungry children than there were the year before.

If you would like a hint of how it would feel to live on the far edge of this widening gap, you could start by having your whole family move into the smallest room in your house or apartment. Then invite your relatives to move their families into the other rooms. Throw out all the furniture except for a cot, a couple of mattresses, a chair, a beat-up radio, and a one-burner hot plate. Get rid of most of your clothes. The refrigerator would have to go too, along with the food in your pantry. Since there would be no indoor plumbing, you would need an old bucket to carry water from the fire hydrant for bathing, drinking, and washing. There's no indoor toilet—in the city everybody shares one in the courtyard, in the country each family uses a chamber pot and empties it outside.

You would not see your father much unless you dropped out of school to help him peddle his wares. Or you might have to stay home to mind the younger children while your mother worked for another family, or begged, or sold little items of food. Just keeping the house clean, doing the sewing and mend-ing, and preparing the food take all day.

Since you would be getting only about a third of the calories and half the protein you need, you would feel tired. You might doze off in school. You would not be able to shake off colds easily. Going to the doctor would involve an all-day wait, at the end of which you still might not have seen him. Then you probably wouldn't be able to afford any medicine.

Records, books, movies? Forget them. You could watch TV on a set in a store window or maybe pay a neighbor to see a show on his set. Since you would not, in this experiment, have time to develop a sense of culture and tradition, you would miss some of the pleasures that people in Latin America's impoverished communities know. You might not have the fortitude that some of them have needed and developed. But you would have an understanding of what is meant by the "gap" between developed and underdeveloped nations, the gulf between rich and poor everywhere.

The population of the United States represents only 1 percent of the world's, but it consumes one-third of the total resources exhausted each year—oil, minerals, food, and energy. The amount of grain used to feed just the cattle raised for slaughter in the United States is four times greater than the amount of grain accessible to other people for all their meats, cereals, flours, gruel, and rice. More than one billion families in the world live on incomes of less than one hundred dollars a year, while the median family income per year in the United States is more than twelve thousand dollars. And within the United States the income is unevenly distributed: the median for black families is only seven thousand dollars a year. Rich as the United States is, children on Indian reservations, in Appalachian mountain hollows, in rural southern communities, and in big city slums suffer from kwashiorkor, the same form of malnutrition that kills children in Africa and Asia. In other words, the economic gap exists in the United States too, demonstrating that plenitude of resources is no guarantee that all benefit from them.

Before Paul and I went to live in Ecuador, it was hard for me to imagine what an underdeveloped country would be like. I knew that people in some countries occasionally demonstrated in front of U.S. embassies. I knew that Nixon had been stoned in Peru and had to be rescued from an angry crowd in Venezuela in 1956. But I didn't understand why.

My social studies teacher in junior high school had taught us that we were the "good neighbors" to the people "south of the border." We were the most generous country in the world and the only one truly committed to freedom and democracy. We gave foreign aid and technological advice, and we invested in industries in those countries. In turn they sold us bananas and coffee, and enriched our music and literature with their rhythms and poetry.

Later I realized the lesson our teacher unconsciously imparted to us. The relationship between the United States and Latin America has nothing to do with being good neighbors. It has everything to do with our demand for their raw materials. The quality of their lives isn't important to us so long as we are guaranteed that coffee and bananas will appear in our supermarkets and copper and tin in our factories.

I realized, too, that I couldn't be a good neighbor to someone if I didn't know much about him, if I didn't care about his problems, share his joys, or respect his traditions and culture. It was pointed out to me and Paul by Mexicans, Ecuadorians, and Cubans alike that we always call ourselves Americans, and call them Latin Americans. But their ancestors were here before ours. Geographically they are just as "American" as we are. Not only have we expropriated for ourselves a name that applies to *two* continents, but we also flaunt our wealth and exercise our power over them. The name, then, is important for the arrogance it signifies. The United States has not been a good neighbor to Latin America; we are the rich folks who live next door: the *norteamericanos*.

This arrogance was something I barely perceived as a high school student in Wellesley, Massachusetts, the setting for the opening pages of this book. Later I saw arrogance operating in the United States itself, in Maryland and Mississippi, where I was a civil rights worker, and in black and Puerto Rican communities in Chicago and New York, where I was a social worker. The authorities I encountered were complacently ignorant about the people they were supposed to be helping and were unwilling to base policies on the human realities of their lives. But it was in Latin America that I saw clearly how much we need to learn and to change. I lived in Juárez, Mexico, as a Peace Corps trainee; I worked in Ecuador as a Peace Corps volunteer; then I visited Cuba as a disillusioned Peace Corps graduate.

This book is a record of my education. I've chosen to describe it just as organically and personally as it occurred—as a series of vignettes about people, events, and communities, with brief excursions into history and politics where they become relevant. Readers may expect these reminiscences of a Peace Corps volunteer to describe how I did my best to change Latin America. Instead, this book is a story of how living in Latin America changed me.

1

Growing Up Yankee

MY AMERICA

I went to high school in the late fifties in Wellesley, Massachusetts, an upper-middle class, white Protestant suburban community. Conservative Republicans dominated the town's politics and culture. Through the united efforts of the real estate agents, no identifiable Jews or Negroes lived there. The small working-class population, mostly Irish and Italian Roman Catholics, lived in clustered sections, tucked out of sight from the large comfortable homes where most people, including my family, lived. The only controversy that I remember ruffling the staid monotony of our town meeting was whether to fluoridate the water supply. The John Birch Society members, fearing the invasion of big government, united with the Christian Scientists, whose religion forbade tampering with natural substances, to defeat the yearly campaign to protect Wellesley's well-orthodontured teeth from decay.

Wellesley blended all the ingredients of the American dream: good schools, a variety of respectable churches, nature walks, clipped lawns, safe streets, and fashionable shops. It offered me a lot. I had close friends, several excellent teachers, and the chance to play tennis and hockey, to swim, to ice skate, to explore on my bike, and to drive our car. The Gamaliel Bradford High School prepared me to succeed academically at one of the nation's best colleges. But I never felt at home there.

Wellesley's values were antithetical to the ones I had grown up with. We had moved there when I was in sixth grade, and it was as if we had arrived in a foreign country. My two sisters and baby brother and I were uprooted from a small community in Alexandria, Virginia, and plopped down amid the children of the "elite," whose parents came from old families or were very rich. Back in Virginia, nobody cared how big your house was, or what your father did, or how you dressed. Nobody fenced off his yard, so we could roam all over, and we called the grown-ups by their first names.

We went to a progressive private school, called Burgundy Farms, because the local public schools were segregated. In my class there were black and white kids, Jews and Gentiles. We always wore blue jeans, and we got to do farm chores. We learned by doing projects and taking field trips, as well as by using workbooks. Girls and boys played together; both learned carpentry and cooking. The teachers helped us to understand each other and not to be cruel. I've never been so happy in school as I was at Burgundy Farms.

In Wellesley it was different. We sat in rows at school, we bowed our heads to repeat mechanically the Lord's Prayer, and we had to memorize "In Flanders Fields" and "The Courtship of Miles Standish." Even in sixth grade, we noticed what clothes the other kids wore, and the "best" children went to Miss Ferguson's dancing class, wearing white gloves.

In Virginia we used to sing, "Whistle while you work, Nixon is a jerk, Eisenhower's going sour, whistle while you work." In Wellesley everybody's parents had voted for Eisenhower in 1952; they all admired Senator Joseph McCarthy.

High school was just as bad. Like most teen-agers I wanted to be popular. I wanted to answer the phone one night and hear the handsomest, smoothest boy in the class ask me for a date. I was always disappointed. I tried to fit into the right mold, but it wasn't my shape. In the first place, I didn't dress right, because my mother had never taught me how. She didn't think clothes should be important. My clothing allowance wasn't enough to let me copy other kids' wardrobes. I'd try to gather hints from the pages of *Seventeen* magazine, but those svelte skinny creatures with flawless complexions and matching accessories seemed to belong to a different species from me.

My other big problem was that I was a good student. That was definitely not cool, especially for a girl. I played down my intelligence, I tried not to talk too much in class, and I never argued with boys. I never told anyone my grades, nor did I admit to having worked on a paper earlier than the night before it was due. In spite of my efforts, I was known as a brain; when the class voted me the best girl student, I was embarrassed. One price I paid for my reputation was having to look for steady boyfriends outside my school.

I was different from my classmates in other ways too. Because of the liberal politics which my parents had taught me, I was completely at odds with the general thinking at school. I was one of three Democrats, and the most outspoken; the other eight hundred students were Republicans or indifferent. I did once manage to get two friends to go to an antinuclear testing meeting, but they were scared to sign a petition demanding a ban on the testing.

Most of my classmates were anti-Semites. In Virginia I had had Jewish friends, but Wellesleyites who didn't know any Jews would tell me that if you let one of "them" move in, "they" would take over the town. They wouldn't listen to my arguments. *The Diary of Anne Frank* was an important book to me. I felt they were insulting Anne, the girl whose courage I admired more than anyone's, and whose death I mourned as though she had been my friend.

I was always aware of Wellesley's smug, cruel sense of superiority. I told myself that I hated its values. I even rebelled in quiet ways. I used to knit socks for my current boyfriend during the Lord's Prayer, and I never pledged allegiance to the flag because it seemed hypocritical to say there's liberty and justice for all in the United States. But I could never overcome my envy of the people my class deemed worthy to wear the enigmatic mantle of "popularity." And I'm afraid I would have gratefully gone with them if they had invited me to their exclusive parties.

And for all my liberalism, I unconsciously shared their prejudice against the children of Wellesley's working class—the policemen, the sanitation men, the custodians, and waitresses. Working-class girls smoked and drank with the boys. They were "fast." Their lipstick was the wrong color. Their tight skirts made them look "cheap." The boys wore tight pants, often pink dungarees, and put clickers on the heels of their shoes. Their hair was long and slicked back into "duck tails," or D.A.'s. Their cars had loud engines. We called the boys hoods. Since they weren't planning on going to college, least of all to our prestigious universities, we thought they were dumb.

According to the "elite's" world view, white middle-class Americans were the culmination of history's logical course of development. Of course we had never studied African, Asian, or American Indian history, nor did we know anything of the history of protest in our own country. We just assumed that we were fit by nature to enjoy the power and the wealth (or to marry men who would wield the power and allocate us our share of the wealth) which our parents' social status had bestowed on us. It was as though we were wearing blinders, cultural blinders that confined our horizons to the borders of the upper-middle-class.

It was easy for us to judge the rest of the world: all we had to do was determine how others would fit into *our* world. Since ours was the center of the universe, we didn't have to think about how we should behave in theirs. That made life comfortably secure. We didn't have to question the morality of a social system that allowed us to enjoy the good life—Shetland sweaters and gold circle pins, cars, college educations, summer camps, trips to Europe—while the majority of the people in this country, for all their hard labor, would never be able to afford them.

OUT OF ONE NEST, INTO A BIGGER ONE

Bryn Mawr was going to be different, I was sure. At a women's college I would be free to be as intellectual as I wanted, without having to worry about what men would think of me. But female sex roles had been deeply ingrained; I still accepted without question the superiority of the male intellect. The professors were Authorities; few dared to dispute them, and I thought those who did were presumptuous. I had friends whose intelligence awed me, but we spent many more hours discussing men than debating ideas or planning careers. Our friendships were close, but we never valued them as much as they deserved. I felt ashamed to spend a Saturday night with a woman friend; a date with almost any male was preferable.

Back then, before the women's movement changed my thinking, I never took myself seriously enough as an active, responsible person. Things would work out somehow; I would always get married. I'd never be forced to define myself.

In many ways college was a confirmation of the social and economic prejudices of high school. Its intensely intellectual atmosphere seemed to exist apart from my personal, inner life.

Classes were an academic challenge which I met fairly successfully, but they didn't help me decide what to do with my life.

FIRST LESSONS IN REALITY

The lessons that are now most relevant to me were taught in a
ghetto of Philadelphia and in a small town on Maryland's
Eastern shore. In November 1962, when I was in my senior year,
I went on a weekend workshop conducted by the American
Friends Service Committee. It was the first time I had ever
walked on the streets of a slum or sat in a black person's living
room. A group of us had been assigned to help an elderly couple
paint their apartment in time for Christmas.

We walked into a small room where two thin, gray-haired old
people were sitting in rocking chairs on either side of the wood
stove that provided the apartment's only heat. The room was
tidy but sparsely furnished. The faded wallpaper showed traces
of a pleasant design of pink flowers. As the old couple watched,
we began to pull off the paper. Plaster crumbled out of holes,
and dozens of roaches scuttled for the nearest cracks. Totally
inexperienced, we dabbed plaster into the holes and slapped dark
green paint onto the walls. The old woman tried to start a conversation, but we couldn't understand her accent, and kept
asking, "Would you repeat that, please?"

The old man lectured the woman. "These young people are
here to help us, so you have to help too." She took up the challenge enthusiastically and slapped brushloads of white paint
across the baseboards, merrily speckling the roaches, and laughed
as they staggered under their new coats. When we left, three-
quarters of the room was painted dark green with a wavy white
trim. I have always wondered whether the painting was ever
finished, and whether the old people were glad it was done.

A FREEDOM MARCH

In April of my senior year I went with my sister Connie and a group of her friends from Swarthmore College to spend a Saturday in Cambridge, Maryland, picketing with a local civil rights group against stores and restaurants that refused to serve black customers. The movement had enraged the local whites; they had attacked several demonstrators during the previous weeks. I was given a can of red pepper to carry on the picket line and nervously watched every approaching dog, ready to dash pepper in its eyes if it lunged. When anybody touched me, I jumped. Dopey jokes made us all laugh hysterically. A backfire cracked like a gunshot.

That evening we went to a mass meeting in a hot, crowded church. Hundreds of people waved their fans rhythmically, stirring the air into little puffs, working just to breathe. They came from all parts of Cambridge's black ward. Teen-agers, young mothers with babies, hefty workmen, old people dressed up for church. We listened to speeches, then joined in freedom songs. Buoyed by the music's spiritual vitality, we moved out in a long column, marching toward the center of town.

Everyone was tense, but the blacks looked calmer and more dignified than we whites did. The teen-aged boys put on their toughest poses, the girls giggled a bit nervously. Strong men looked warily from side to side. The old people walked slowly, some with canes, their heads held high. Everyone was singing loudly. The white people who lined our route cursed, jeered, and threatened. They nourished a special rage for the white civil rights workers. A young woman in Bermuda shorts and a red sweater leaned out to scream at me, "Go home nigger lover." With her blond ponytail, she looked like any American teen-ager, but hatred made her distorted face hideous.

Curses weren't dangerous. It was the blacks who took the real risks. They weren't going back to college when the march was over. They couldn't leave their homes and children behind. Their employers could fire them, and snipers could shoot them at night. Their churches could be bombed, and no Cambridge cop would ever catch the bomber.

Outside the courthouse we huddled together in a large circle. As the minister prayed to the Lord to help us in our struggle for freedom, we looked out for rocks from the angry ring of whites surrounding us. The church, which had seemed so strange when we first arrived, felt like a wonderful home when we finally got back to it. The freedom songs vibrated with extra passion. We had all faced our fear and survived that round together.

We laughed all the way back to college, finally releasing our tension. I knew that the day had changed my life. It revealed a frontier to me, one that I had only glimpsed in newspaper accounts of freedom rides. Here people were putting their lives on the front line in the battle for justice. The territory was completely unknown to me, but the day's events made me want to explore it.

LIVING ON A THREATENED FRONTIER

Connie and I went back to spend our summer vacation in Cambridge. We had been asked by the Cambridge Non-Violent Action Committee to run a tutorial program for black children who might enter the white schools in the fall. Driving down Route 50 in Maryland, we passed a large caravan of lumbering brown National Guard trucks, loaded with troops on their way to Cambridge. The tensions of spring had flared into open violence. White vigilantes were staging night raids. They had been shooting at black people's homes and cars. The blacks were beginning to shoot back.

The governor mobilized the National Guard to patrol the border (ironically named Race Street after an early race track there) between the black and white sections to keep people from killing each other. Our battered old station wagon, loaded with books, was about to enter a war zone.

The troops were efficient in their patrols, but they couldn't be everywhere. Everyone lived with the anticipation of an explosion. We had to be inside before the 10:00 P.M. curfew. Somewhere out in the dark, we'd hear a rifle crack. After the first few nights in this strange, occupied town, I stopped crying myself to sleep. Nevertheless, I was glad that Connie and I shared the same room.

It wasn't only the soldiers who made Cambridge frightening at first. It was the new customs, the new ways of speech, the new people. We were living with Mr. and Mrs. Jackson. The first Sunday breakfast Mrs. Jackson served us fried bologna, and I gagged because it was so greasy. The loud gospel music from the radio was so different from the church music I knew. People were very polite, but I felt awkwardly stiff with my careful Wellesley diction and my reserved formality. When the Jacksons and their friends talked they merged anger and humor in rapid, relaxed, slangy sentences. They shared jokes that I couldn't even get. When the conversation came around to "white folks," I was never sure how tainted I was by my color. Would they ever accept me?

I gradually learned to relax. They who lived on a threatened frontier taught me to take life easier, to laugh at the ridiculousness of so much that was going on. I grew to love the food, the music, the church services, and the mass meetings. I especially enjoyed being with the kids in our tutorial classes, but most of all I loved sitting around talking.

Addie Jackson and her husband Freddy took a great risk when they offered to put us up. They jeopardized their jobs, even their lives. Their jobs didn't pay much, but at least they both had work. Mrs. Jackson picked the meat from boiled ("berled" it was pronounced) crabs in a small factory; Mr. Jackson emptied baskets of tomatoes into vats of steaming water at another canning plant. For Sunday dinner we often got to taste delicacies slipped from the assembly lines: homemade crab cakes and fresh tomatoes.

The Jacksons lived in a small wooden house. We would sit on the front porch in the evenings, drinking iced tea and talking with Mrs. Jackson and her neighbors. Mr. Jackson watched TV in the living room, laughing at the comedies, cheering the wrestling matches. Connie and I used to think that he imagined himself a wrestler, flipping his wife around the ring. She was much larger than he, and she tended to boss him around.

Mrs. Jackson would tell us about her job, about the white folks she used to work for. With great relish she passed on the gossip about the white part of town as well as the black. We talked about the mass meetings and the freedom marches. She asked how our classes were going and questioned us sharply about which people we were making friends with. She didn't like some of the no-account young men hanging around the periphery of the freedom movement, and she told us not to talk to them. She particularly disliked Jesse Lee Jones, an alcoholic ex-Marine whom I happened to like a lot. She also scolded us if we got back too close to the curfew. She considered herself our mother for the summer.

She agreed with the organizers that the movement's goals should be more than the integration of restaurants. "What good does it do you to be able to sit at a lunch counter if you ain't got the money to buy a hamburger?" she'd ask. "Our peoples needs jobs, and they ain't none here now."

A quiet woman, very ordinary, very determined, but not rhetorical. To support the boycott against the white businesses downtown, she joined a car pool to travel forty miles to Salisbury to do her weekly shopping. Despite the inconvenience and the extra cost, she was determined to continue the boycott until the white stores downtown hired blacks.

That was one of the happiest summers of my life. I felt useful. I felt part of a growing movement of "black and white together." With this new-found strength, I could change the United States. The climax of the summer's activities was the March on Washington. Two hundred thousand of us filled the Mall by the Lincoln Memorial. We heard Martin Luther King, Jr.'s, famous speech. "I Have a Dream," he preached. We did too.

AN INTRODUCTION TO "THE WELFARE"

In the fall of 1963 I drove out to start graduate school in social work at the University of Chicago. Stopping to drop Connie off for her last year at Swarthmore, I discovered that a young writer, Paul Cowan, who had spent most of the summer in Cambridge, was also driving to Chicago. Paul and I took turns following each other along the monotonous, endless turnpikes. As the journey went on, we spent more and more time in the Howard Johnsons, turning necessary coffee breaks into long, wide-ranging discussions. By the time we reached Chicago, we had fallen in love.

Graduate school, it turned out, was even more frustrating than college. My classes were superficial and dull; they turned a rich complicated world into a series of pat phrases and flat case studies. Paul's classes in the Committee on Social Thought were intellectually stimulating, but they were so remote from the community we lived in that they didn't hold his interest at all.

Outside class, Paul and I saw dozens of movies, ate at little restaurants, went to parties, and made new friends. We also joined the Chicago civil rights movement, working with The Woodlawn Organization (T.W.O.), which was organizing the residents of Paul's block, most of whom were black. The tenants of Paul's building organized a rent strike to force the landlady to make repairs. The block club picketed the corner grocery store that was underweighing and overpricing. We won permission from the university to build a playground on an empty lot and collected money to buy materials. We worked very hard, but the playground never got finished. It was too big a job—the block club couldn't raise enough money to finish or enlist enough people to help. The community was disappointed. Once again, things hadn't worked out for them. When Paul and I left for the Mississippi Freedom Summer Project to register voters in the South, some of the neighbors gossiped that we had stolen the playground's funds. That rumor hurt. It also showed us the dangers of promising more than you can deliver.

The people I worked with taught me more than my professors did. My classes neither explained the reality I was experiencing in my field work nor provided the tools to deal with it. For my field practice, I was a caseworker in a ghetto office of the Cook County Department of Welfare.

My first client was an unmarried mother of twelve. She raised her family in a six-room apartment in a crumbling tenement on one of Chicago's most dangerous blocks. The house was always absolutely neat, the beds folded up in the hall, the children very quiet and well behaved. One day in January she showed me her kitchen closet—packed solid with ice from a burst pipe. Through her, I saw the absurd, self-defeating stinginess of the welfare policies. For one, they wouldn't give her enough money to buy a washing machine so she spent lots of money each week at a laundromat.

My supervisor told me that my goals were to get Mrs. Smith into a better apartment and help her decide not to have a thirteenth child. The first task was impossible because no landlord would rent to a woman on welfare with twelve children. She had been on the waiting list for years to get into a public housing project, but there were still no vacancies.

I couldn't persuade Mrs. Smith that any method of birth control was safe; she'd heard bad stories about all of them. She didn't particularly trust me, partly because I was young, white, and childless, but mostly because I was from the welfare department. She didn't want any worker telling her how to run her life. Her experience with us was that we cared only about ways to cut her check.

All I could do was to search through the endless pages of welfare regulations, hoping to find provisions that would allow me to apply for special increases—for another bed, so that each child would have his own, or for clothing for school.

The welfare system was keeping the Smith family alive. It was not, however, providing them with enough money to eat nutritiously, dress with pride, have any entertainment, or feel optimistic about their future. Mrs. Smith could not work outside her home; her job in the apartment was more than full-time. She should have been a professor at the School of Social Services Administration, teaching how to manage a home, feed twelve children on a budget that allowed her sixty cents a day per person for food, and nurture a spirit of family loyalty. Instead, she was on a treadmill. As her caseworker, I was only helping that treadmill creak on. I began to wonder if being a social worker would ever enable me to help anyone.

The welfare was my first experience with a truly inhuman bureaucracy. Paul and I were also becoming active in the effort to stop a somewhat bigger one—the Pentagon. In those early days of the antiwar movement, we stayed up late every night, helping to organize teach-ins against the war in Vietnam. We believed that if only we could convince enough people that the war was based on mistaken policies and assumptions, we could end it. We were part of the most exciting and humane group of people we've ever worked with. Our last year in Chicago, 1965, sped by. When school ended, we decided it was time to move on.

NEW YORK

After two years in Chicago, Paul and I decided to get married. We would start our life together back east. The wedding took place under a wide-branching butternut tree on my uncle's farm in Massachusetts. My ancestors had come from New England, and it was important to take this new step in my life from a place where I had roots. Our friends and relatives sat in a circle as we spoke our vows to each other.

We were still on our honeymoon when we read that President Johnson had called for escalation of the war in Vietnam, and had ended draft deferments for married men. Paul was suddenly eligible. For days we discussed our alternatives. He did not want to join the army. We were both convinced the war was immoral: our government was supporting a corrupt dictator against the wishes of the people. But we didn't want to move to Canada, Paul didn't want to go to jail, and we thought it was a cop-out to feign symptoms for a psychological deferment. Our choices narrowed down to one—the Peace Corps. In college we had both been excited by the idea of volunteering to work overseas. When we got back to New York we sent in our application to the Peace Corps.

Meanwhile Paul started as a reporter for the *Village Voice*, and I got a job at a settlement house in our neighborhood. I was to work with a Puerto Rican tenants' group that was organizing a rent strike on its block. The U.S. Post Office owned all the buildings, which it planned to tear down to enlarge the main branch. In the meantime, the buildings were deteriorating. We became the first group ever to picket the post office for being a slumlord.

Starting that job I confronted a whole new set of stereotypes. In Wellesley, Spanish had been considered a language for people "not bright enough" to learn French. I never saw or heard a Puerto Rican, yet I had vivid images of them: sallow-faced greasy men with switchblades or lazy, happy-go-lucky people with lives composed of *señoritas*, *siestas*, and always *mañana*.

I had never known a Latin American. I couldn't tell the difference between a Puerto Rican, an Ecuadorian, and a Mexican. My job changed all that. The members of the tenants' organization accepted me so warmly, despite my total ignorance of their language, that I immediately wanted to know them better. Now I longed to learn Spanish. The words flowed so rapidly, so humorously, so passionately.

People would frequently invite me to stay for a cup of strong sweet coffee. Francisco Pérez and his wife would talk to me for hours in their kitchen. Francisco was a doorman uptown; his wife kept the house, watched the three children, and cooked. They loved the neighborhood. The school was good and integrated both economically and racially. The subway was close by, the streets were safe, the park attractive, and the supermarkets offered good bargains. Their apartment was too small for them, but the rent was low.

If the post office demolished their building, Francisco and his family would have to leave the community. They would be able to afford to live only in some distant neighborhood, with poor schools, less convenient transportation, and dangerous streets.

Five months later, sad to leave my friends in the middle of their fight, I said good-by. The Peace Corps had accepted us for a community development project in Ecuador. The training program was about to begin at the University of New Mexico.

In 1968 I went back to see if any of my friends were still living on the block. I saw only a muddy lot surrounded by a high link fence. It was a parking lot for empty postal trucks. In 1975, it was the same—Francisco's children could have grown up on that block.

2

The Peace Corps at Home

AN INTERNATIONAL SIT-IN

In 1965 thousands of people like Paul and me were working in the civil rights movement. Several top officials of the Peace Corps decided to try to enlist that enthusiastic commitment. They were frequently rebuffed. By that time most of us had become disillusioned and suspicious of our government's intentions. In the south and in urban ghettoes we had seen only token inroads made against racial and economic injustice. We knew, too, that napalm was burning innocent Vietnamese peasants. Paul and I accepted the Peace Corps's offer mostly because we could think of no better way to avoid the draft. I was sure that the Peace Corps existed more to create a friendly, generous image for the United States than to provide assistance to Africa, Asia, or Latin America.

Paul was more optimistic. He thought that when we got out to some village somewhere we might be able to do something useful. Besides, he was anxious to have a new adventure. Since we both felt we owed our country some form of service, we decided to give the Peace Corps a try. At least we'd be working for peace, not war.

Paul interviewed two prominent Peace Corps officials for an article in the *Village Voice*, and came back full of enthusiasm. Frank Mankiewicz, who had been Peace Corps director in Peru, and would later become an adviser to Robert Kennedy and George McGovern, described the Peace Corps as an "international sit-in." He wrote: "The ultimate aim of a community development project is nothing less than complete change, reversal —or revolution if you wish—in the social and economic conditions of the countries to which we are accredited."

As Peace Corps director in Ethiopia, Harris Wofford had developed an enticing concept of the Peace Corps as a "university in dispersion." He described it as a "university of seminars, workshops, organized readings, and always and continually a dialogue with the other volunteers and host country friends where the talk would be open, expansive, and long into the night."

Paul's interviews convinced us that the Peace Corps would provide an exciting venture and not simply the least undesirable alternative to the draft. Although we wondered whether we as foreigners could accomplish much in a strange country—let alone make a revolution—we assumed that the local people who were organizing this international sit-in had asked for our help. We wanted to believe we were going to do something important and useful. We wanted to believe that we were needed.

Paul and I argued for weeks over which project to choose, mulling over one exotic country after another. We were first tempted to go off to a remote Pacific island, then to spend two years absorbing Eastern culture in Nepal. But the warm acceptance I'd received from Francisco and the other Puerto Rican tenants on the block in New York drew my interest to Latin America. There were strong practical arguments for going to Latin America as well: since those countries are the closest to us we should learn about them before traveling farther afield.

Since so many Spanish-speaking people live in New York, we would be able to bring what we learned in the Peace Corps back to our neighborhood.

Paul was finally persuaded to accept my choice when Mankiewicz told him that a community development project just being organized for Guayaquil was considered "the hottest thing going" in the Peace Corps. If selected, we would join other highly qualified "blue ribbon" trainees to prepare to work as administrators in the city hall and as community organizers in the *barrios suburbanos*, the communities where half a million of Ecuador's poorest people lived. Some of us would be placed in the city planning office, others in public works, budgeting, marketing, or community development. We would not only try to teach our colleagues to be more effective public servants, but we would also intervene with them on behalf of our neighbors in the barrios. Our goal was to help city hall provide more effective municipal services to the city's neglected poor. Our project director, the man who hatched the plan, would later tell us that our work "could mean the difference between peaceful revolution and bloodshed in Guayaquil."

PLEASE WEAR YOUR NAME TAGS

The next two years loomed mysteriously ahead as we boarded the Santa Fe Superchief for Albuquerque in February of 1966. We were already leaving America behind, at least the America we knew. The journey across flat cornfields and empty plains, with nighttime stops in nameless little stations, then through the Rockies—all glimpsed from our snug berths and our white-clothed table in the dining car—was a magical interlude. We were suspended in time and space between two worlds.

The first memo handed us by the training staff dissipated the magic. Our new world, it turned out, was a variation on the old world of high school. "Trainees must attend all classes and all assigned activities," read the mimeographed sheet,

> and are expected to have sufficient sense of personal responsibility to arrive on time to all scheduled meetings. If you are unavoidably late to a class you will be expected to explain your tardiness to the instructor after that class. Should you miss a class, please inform the instructor of the reason at the earliest possible opportunity.

> Every one of your instructors will contribute to your total assessment, inasmuch as the training program is part of the selection process which began before you came here and will continue after you leave. Please wear your name tags to all training functions.

Punctuality and good attendance were thus established as the basic qualifications for acceptance into the Peace Corps. With our instructors "assessing" us, we all quickly understood that it would be risky to challenge them or to complain about irrelevant lectures. Dutifully we attended classes in history, community development, health, and current events. We passed the boring hours by doodling, playing tick-tack-toe, or writing letters home.

We had to rise at six thirty each morning to go to physical education class in time to get in a healthy dose of set-ups and an endurance run up and down the stadium bleachers before classes began at eight thirty. The air was thin at that altitude, and I often felt nauseated after the workout. We also took an overnight hike up a snowy mountain and learned to rappel down rock cliffs. We were drown-proofed, which meant that we could stay afloat for twenty minutes with our hands and feet tied. The theory behind this rugged program was that we would become better people for overcoming its challenges. If we set our sights high enough, they said, we would grow tall to meet them.

I was proud of the shape I got into, but those skills never served any purpose in Guayaquil. The city wasn't remotely close to any mountain, and it was too hot to run about in. Besides, the people would have thought us mad.

The one bright spot in the program was the Spanish language instruction. We spent five hours a day in class with dedicated, competent teachers who had all grown up in Spain or Latin America. After two months, we could converse with some degree of fluency.

A BLUE-RIBBON GROUP

Once we had come to know most of our fellow trainees, we couldn't figure out why we were considered such a talented group. A third of us had graduate degrees or had worked in city government, but only a few had ever been community organizers. Almost nobody had lived for long outside his or her white middle-class environment.

The group had come to Albuquerque from all over the United States, recent college graduates for the most part. The trainees were friendly, eager to like one another, although the good-natured bantering which dominated our meetings often covered up hostility. Sometimes people became nasty. They nicknamed one member "Batman" because he had gone to a masquerade in that costume soon after we got to training. They mocked him for his eccentricities, like carrying a hip bag full of colored pens. He used the colors to take notes, for he was dyslectic and couldn't read well. They never bothered to figure him out or to enjoy his comments. The guys would call out "Hey, Batman!" in high-pitched voices; the girls would giggle at him.

And, like the kids I went to high school with, the trainees were anti-intellectual. They made fun of Paul for talking so intensely, for pursuing disagreements with the instructors, and for referring to books he had read. Although I felt older than most of them, they still made me feel socially inadequate, just as I used to feel in high school. I couldn't giggle or be clever. I couldn't defer to "the guys."

They reminded me of my high school classmates in another way. They went along with the mocking jokes that one of the most popular trainees frequently directed at the three Jewish trainees. He called one of them a "little Yid"—all in good fun, of course—and made fun of the Seder which another trainee organized at Passover. One of the staff members criticized Paul's "abrasive, big-city personality," by which he meant that Paul acted like a pushy Jew.

This sort of mocking was directed at anybody who didn't conform. The competitiveness of our situation reinforced the need for conformity. We each felt under scrutiny by the program's staff and by each other. We were required to rate the other trainees on special sheets, listing those who we thought would make good volunteers and those who would not. We drew perverse satisfaction from noting one another's weaknesses. Gossip comforted us, for the signs of another's inadequacies reinforced our hopes that we were faring better.

THE AMERICAN WAY

It was easy to criticize the training program. We all griped about the boring classes, the petty regulations, the incompetent staff. It was harder, though, to perceive the central weakness of the program. That insight came after we got into the field.

The instructors outlined a simple methodology for organizing a community, but they failed to help us prepare for the psychological task of living and working as outsiders. We knew that organizing couldn't be as simple as the way our teachers described it, even though they did try to illustrate some potential pitfalls by recounting tales of their own experiences as Peace Corps volunteers.

To prepare us adequately to face the problems they should have anticipated we would have, they would have had to challenge the fundamental assumption on which the Peace Corps is based. That premise is that virtually any North American of good will can enter any community and expect to be able to organize its people for whatever goal we would help them choose. Because a community is poor, it needs our assistance. Our trainers never questioned that assumption; none of us did until after we'd been in Guayaquil.

They did not challenge the cultural blinders we all brought with us. One day in a film about community development in East Africa, we saw a carpenter who kept nails in the tight curls of his hair. When he reached up to pull out a nail to hammer, the group started laughing. Our trainers didn't stop the film to discuss why we couldn't accept the man's work habits.

The group's complacency was based on the members' belief that the American way is the best way. After spending five days living with a Mexican-American family in Martíneztown, one of the barrios of Albuquerque, I wrote home:

> One girl just told me that she had not enjoyed herself at all. She says she doesn't like poor people. But she isn't alone. Last week another girl said, "You can take a person out of the slum, but you can't take the slum out of a person."
>
> Another time in community development class a trainee said, "You know we are the most generous people in the world. America is the only country in the history of mankind that has ever tried to solve the problem of poverty."

Whether they wanted to make a revolution or just to teach one Ecuadorian how to embroider a doily, the trainers and trainees all assumed that Ecuador was a blank mass of needy people waiting for our help. One of our trainers stated it bluntly. He had worked for the U.S. government in Guayaquil as a consultant to city hall for two years. He had been one of the planners of our project. When I asked him how our relatively unskilled group could serve a useful function in the *municipio*, or city government, he told me, "When you get there you'll realize that your background is the important thing you're bringing, the training you have absorbed just from living in the United States. These people will follow the example you set. Here's an illustration: I always observed when I worked there that if a man had ten pieces of paper on his desk he'd make ten trips to the wastebasket to throw them all out. Now I know that all of you would make only one trip. That's the kind of efficiency you'll teach, sometimes without knowing it."

The trainers didn't challenge the trainees' arrogance; they shared it. Their descriptions of their experiences did not prepare us to appreciate the complexity of people's lives or the strengths of their culture and traditions. They didn't inspire us to open ourselves to the value of other peoples' uniqueness because they saw the Peace Corps more as a romantic adventure than a psychologically profound experience. They expected that our experience would and should repeat theirs: parties, drinking, dancing; long committee meetings, where the forces of responsible citizenship take power over neighborhoods; new foods; and exotic vacations. They told us how to boil our water to sterilize it, how to bargain in the marketplace, and how to travel inexpensively.

I wish we had explored different questions. Like: What were the political implications of the work we were about to do? Mankiewicz called it revolutionary; the Peace Corps director in Guayaquil also talked about "peaceful revolution." But what is a revolution? What revolutions can we study, learn from? Can foreigners be revolutionaries? What was the role of the U.S.

government in Ecuador? Was it helpful or harmful, and to whom? Would people resent us? Were we part of our government's aid program, or were we distinct? What happens to outsiders who go to live in foreign communities, especially ones who go to "help"? What feelings could we expect to have?

We didn't delve into any of those questions. Instead we were indoctrinated with what amounted to the Peace Corps's excuse for the inevitable confusion, fears, and loneliness we would experience as foreigners in Ecuador. They called it "culture shock." According to the psychiatrists who lectured us, culture shock is a universal reaction felt by people in new surroundings. If we found ourselves lonely, depressed, or angry it would be because we would be adrift in an environment where people didn't understand the signals we sent out and we didn't understand the messages they were sending us. The doctors showed us graphs that indicated when this phase would be likely to hit us. They warned us to counteract it by plunging into activity rather than withdrawing; to accept it as normal and wait for it to pass.

Culture shock accounts for a certain emotional cycle that many volunteers experience. The concept does not, however, take into consideration the political and social realities that affect even more deeply the way volunteers may feel. What if a volunteer finds her work meaningless? Or what if another is sent to a community that does not want him? What if the Peace Corps has led yet another to believe that she will be helping people, and she discovers that she isn't? We left training wearing the armor of "culture shock" to defend us against future depression. It would turn out to be more of an excuse than a solace.

If the Peace Corps training program was any indication, we would never participate in an "international sit-in," however figuratively Mankiewicz meant it. We who hoped to organize Ecuadorians to change conditions that oppressed them were too frightened to organize ourselves to change the training program which angered most of us.

Nor did the "university in dispersion" seem likely to material-ize. Only a handful of trainees had any interest in talking long into the night. They preferred poker, gossip, and jokes. If the reality of the Peace Corps turned out to be as different from the official rhetoric as training had proved to be, we were in for two disappointing years. Paul and I began to talk about quitting.

Only at the end of training, after final selection, did we call a meeting to bring our criticisms to the staff. One of our biggest complaints was that the leaders had allowed us no role in plan-ning or evaluating the training program. We told them that it was absurd to prepare us for working on our own by treating us like children.

3

Living in Mexico

TORTILLAS AND BEANS

"Bluebird," a shabby blue bus with hard narrow seats, carried our Peace Corps training group from Albuquerque to Juárez, just over the border in Mexico. It had rattled for hours across the flat arid plains before turning off the El Paso expressway in Texas. We went over a modern cement bridge above the Rio Grande, which was disappointingly small for an international boundary. It was May 1966, and Juárez was to be our home for the next month. Living here was to be the most important part of our training.

It had just stopped raining. The cobbled streets shone wetly. The buildings gleamed. We could see the skyscrapers of El Paso behind us, but we now were obviously in a foreign city. The streets were lined with brightly painted concrete buildings, sometimes lace-edged with balconies.

In the modest hotel that was to be the group's headquarters we met with the Peace Corps staff members who would supervise us. We would live with families in the outlying *colonias,* or suburbs, they said, but would come downtown every morning for Spanish classes and discussions of what we were learning about community development. We were to devote the afternoons and evenings to learning as much as we could about our colonia.

We were handed a slip of paper bearing the name Domingo Martínez and an address in the colonia Emiliano Zapata. Finding him was our first challenge. First we had to get to the bus— it wasn't too hard to ask the way, but it took several tries before we could understand the answer. Then the dilapidated orange bus jolted over holes, labored up hills, and stopped at every corner. After we got off we wandered through the muddy streets of the colonia, looking for the Martínezes' block. By this time it was dark. We finally knocked on a simple, unpainted door.

Señora Paula Martínez invited us into a small room. The only light came from a flickering kerosene lantern. There were three beds in the room, and small children, pressed shyly back against the wall, sat on all of them. Señor Martínez shook our hands and gestured for us to sit down. What to talk about as total strangers, literally in the dark, with a language problem? Their Spanish was fast and colloquial; ours slow, ungrammatical, and badly pronounced.

We did manage to understand the Señora's offer of *café*. Shortly thereafter something from those long hours of language practice filtered its way back into my scattered brain, and we began a halting conversation about the weather and the children. We all agreed that the rain was refreshing after the heat, but the mud was not. We learned the names and ages of the five children: Ismaela, eleven; Socorro, nine; Pepe, five; Cuquita, three; and Teresita, two. Paula's sixth baby was due in two months. We had no children, we explained, because we'd only been married several months; and yes, we thought we would have some, but not for a few years.

The children sat still and silent at first. Gradually they wriggled closer. Then unable to control their impulses, they started to giggle. "¡*Qué manera más rara de hablar!*" one of them whispered. "What a strange way to talk!" Socorro, a thin, dark-haired girl with a wide mischievous smile, moved closer to Paul. He made a funny tongue-clacking sound. She laughed and tried to copy him. The others drew closer too.

For several hours we maintained this sort of awkward conversation while we waited for the Peace Corps trainer to deliver our suitcase and cots. He didn't come. At last, the Martínezes politely offered us one of their beds. We climbed in with our clothes on, after Pepe had shown us the way to the outhouse in back, and the family divided itself between the other two beds. That made nine of us in a nine-by-twelve-foot room.

By suppertime the next day, we were Pablo *y* Raquel; they were Mingo, Paula, and five special children. Our cots finally arrived, and Paula offered us the other room for ourselves. She warned us to put the wooden shutter over the window at night so that nobody could climb in. The only other furniture in the room was an ice chest, from which Paula sold cold sodas to the neighbors, and a wooden box. The air was dusty from the dirt floor and smelled unpleasantly of kerosene whenever Paula cooked. The next morning we woke to find Socorro and Pepe tugging at our sheets and tickling our feet.

It took a while for us to feel comfortable with one another as friends rather than as specimens. They found us strange and amusing: we were the biggest, whitest people who had ever been in their house. The children mimicked our dreadful accents, and teased when we didn't know the words for everyday things like apron or frying pan or hammer. Paul joked with Paula about *perros calientes*, the literal translation for hot dogs. He told her they were the most popular food at home, and she was horrified that people would eat dogs. The Martínezes spiced their beans with hot green chili peppers. Socorro's game was to dare us to put more and more *chile* on our food. She would laugh uproariously as we gasped and choked, tears running down our cheeks. Then she'd run to the ice chest for sodas to quench the fires in our throats.

We were also an economic boon to the Martínezes. The two dollars fifty a day we paid for room and board was more than they had ever earned. Paula could buy meat each day, a luxury which she could normally afford only once a week. She saved the rest of the money to pay for wiring the house to the electric line the city was just extending up to the colonia. For the first time the Martínezes would have an electric light in their front room.

As our friendship developed we talked about more complicated things. Mingo and Paul sometimes joked about drinking and fantasized about going downtown without their wives. Mingo unfolded the colonia's history and explained the different political factions that contended within it. Mingo didn't talk with me at any length, partly because politics wasn't considered a women's interest and partly because it wasn't thought proper to talk alone with another man's wife.

He and Paula told us how they had come to Juárez from small villages near Torreón, four hundred miles south down the main highway. Mingo's mother still lived a six-hour walk from the nearest bus stop. Their parents were peasants, working long hours every day in their small fields. Rising before dawn, bending over the brown soil and the green pinto bean plants under the baking sun till late afternoon, the men and boys could raise only enough crops to feed the family and trade in town. Some of the children went to work for tiny wages on larger farms nearby. They could never harvest enough to sell a surplus in the market. The women and girls arose even earlier. They worked all day cleaning the house, washing the clothes, and preparing the food. It took hours to grind the corn, boil it, and shape it into tortillas. Tortillas and beans was what they ate. Always tortillas and beans.

During the long days of those long hard years, Paula and

Mingo decided to leave their families and head north. They'd heard that in Juárez you could get papers to work in the States, where the money came easy. If not, Juárez would surely offer more than the farm, where they could never hope for a life any easier than their parents'. In rural Mexico, the peasants do not own enough land to plant large crops. Nor can they get loans to buy seeds for new crops, fertilizer, or pesticides. They grow only enough to feed themselves, and if the weather turns bad, they go hungry.

Like small drops Paula and Mingo each joined the rushing stream of people flowing north. They met in Juárez, where Mingo had found a job loading blocks of ice at a factory. They married and lived in a tiny room downtown until they decided to join a group of people planning to move up onto the empty land behind the city. Overnight, dozens of families built a community of wooden and cardboard shacks. The wealthy dairy farmer who owned the unused land called out his guards, but the people fought them off. The city government decided they could stay.

Paula and Mingo gradually transformed their shack: with adobe bricks molded from wet mud and straw, they built a one-room house, then added on. They planted some cacti out back. The young leaves are called *nopalitos* and are good to eat. Their garden began with bean plants, then corn and squash. Mingo added a lean-to behind where Paula could cook. He dug a deep hole for the outhouse.

Their neighbors worked just as hard. Under the hot noon sun, when our stereotypes show every Mexican deep in siesta, the men are out improving their houses: patching the roof, adding a room, building a chicken house, making a toy for the children, cementing a floor, or planting a tree.

Little by little, the colonia grew from a shanty town to a neighborhood. The bus route was extended from downtown, a large church and a new school were erected, and a water main installed. The Martínezes got a spigot in their front yard. Finally there was electricity. The colonia was no longer on the town's outer limits. Miles of dirt roads, blocks of adobe houses stretched up the sides of the arid mountain behind it.

A WOMAN'S LIFE

Since her late teens, Paula had been caring for children. She had lived through hard times I could barely imagine, and my life back home was just as psychologically remote to her. But we slowly became friends. The bond that we shared as women built a sturdy bridge across the gap between our cultures and our languages. We respected each other and enjoyed talking and laughing together.

Paula was of medium height with bronze skin, high cheek-bones, and a proud Indian nose. Her dark hair was tied back in a ponytail. Her eyes gave her face an unusual intensity; they could never hide what she was feeling inside. They sparkled when the family sat around joking together. They concentrated steadily on the people with whom she talked, occasionally glinting with puzzlement or concern. When she sat alone though, they were often tense beneath her furrowed brow. She was calm but always poised against some new threat to her family.

We would talk about her hopes for her children. Though she loved them all deeply, she didn't want any more. It seemed odd to her—unnatural, in fact—that I should want to postpone having a baby, but she was curious to know how I avoided getting pregnant. She had never heard of birth control until I told her about the pills I was taking. Paula said she would ask about birth control for herself when she went to the clinic to have the baby. Six would be enough children. She didn't see how they could afford another.

47

From her I learned how happy children can make a mother. The kids not only helped Paula with the chores, but they joked with her, teased her, confided in her, and needed her. I hoped my family would be as loving as hers.

I also learned how poverty hovers as a constant threat to a family's security and happiness. Several years before Mingo had lost his job at the ice factory and could find no other work. He started to drink. He'd leave in the morning to find work and come home late at night blind drunk. He frightened the children and Paula too.

To feed the family, Paula started selling fruit in the marketplace. Rising before dawn, she'd walk with three children down to the plaza, carrying cuca in a shawl across her back. There she'd buy a sack of oranges and tomatoes from the wholesaler. Arranging her wares in piles on a mat, she'd sit all morning haggling with the customers over the price of each fruit. Then she'd walk back home with the children. The bus cost too much.

Those terrible days were over. Mingo had stopped drinking a couple of years ago. Still, she could never rest easy. Whenever he was late she worried. The Martínezes had no cushion between today's survival and tomorrow's hunger.

Paula gently drew me into her daily routine. She taught me how to cook beans, boil the corn for the tortillas, and select the best cactus leaves. I offered to help with the washing and ironing, but I was more of a hindrance than help. It was too hard to get my clothes clean with a tub and scrub board—I gave up and settled for grimy shirts. The iron was also difficult—I had to heat it on the stove and then iron quickly so as not to burn the clothes. Then I reheated it. All these tasks I was used to whisking through took hours.

I liked best to go with Maela to the store or with Socorro to the mill. The front room of a neighbor's house, the store was always full of people. The women had to go there several times a day because they never had enough money to buy corn or coffee or sugar in large quantities, and they did not have refrigerators to keep milk or cheese fresh. They relied on the *tienda* as a place to meet people and catch up on news and gossip. They liked the break from the isolation of their own houses.

The mill was about half a mile from the house. We'd walk the hilly, dusty road carrying the bucket of corn between us, neatly covered with a clean cloth. The people brought the dusty browns of the colonia's roads, houses, and yards vividly to life. Children whistled and shouted as they played around their houses. On days when it rained, they splashed in the large puddles. They turned old tires into all kinds of toys. Women hung out their laundry and called to the children to come and run an errand. Dogs barked, little groups of chickens pecked in backyards.

At the mill a long line of children wound back. They laughed and fought and pushed as they waited to enter the shed. Finally it would be Socorro's turn to pour her corn into the hopper of the sputtering, clanking grinder. *Splat!* The *masa*, or tortilla dough, spattered out the other end. She would scrape it up and put her *centavos* into the miller's oily calloused hand.

When we got home, Paula would spend the next hour pressing the masa into thin circles. She cooked them on an ungreased griddle, then wrapped them in a clean cloth to stay warm for lunch. She could have bought tortillas at a nearby factory, but Mingo preferred the ones she made. When she was a girl, Paula told me, she had to sit by the fire all during the meal to keep hot tortillas coming for the men and boys. Only after they'd finished did she have a chance to eat.

Noon meal was the biggest. Mingo would come home around one; Maela would be back from the morning shift at school. Socorro and Pepe would have eaten early before the second shift began. We'd have noodle soup, beans, a small piece of meat or cheese, rice, tortillas, and green chili. Several times Paula made *chiles rellenos*, green peppers stuffed with cheese, dipped in egg batter and fried. They were my favorite. Breakfast had been beans and tortillas; supper would be the same.

The only modern appliance in the house was the radio, which was an old portable model. It lightened the day's chores. As for women everywhere, the *novelas*, or soap operas, which the colonia listened to were fantasies to relieve reality—the heroines had worse troubles, or at least more exotic ones. Paula and the children knew the plots of all the different stories; they carefully followed their favorite characters through good times and bad. Sometimes they shouted at the villain, or wept for the heroine. Walking down the street, you could hear the over-dramatic voices of the actors from almost every house. The bouncy rhythm of the Fanta orange soda commercials was part of the colonia's melody.

Supper was another pleasant time. By then the air had cooled, and the breeze blew fresh. We'd sit around the wooden kitchen table, our faces shining in the soft, flickering light of the kerosene lamp. Since there were only four tin plates we waited for the younger children to eat first. Then Mingo would gather little Teresa onto his lap, and Paula would serve his meal. She always waited till last to eat. The older children recounted the day's adventures at school, or repeated the latest neighborhood gossip. They all quizzed us on the newest words they had taught us and sometimes asked questions about the United States. How far away did our families live? Was it easy to find a job there? Was it true that the government took better care of poor people than the Mexican government does? Where was the war being fought? Mingo made shadow creatures on the wall and Paul and I taught the kids to play tick-tack-toe.

Then everybody went to bed. As I wriggled about in search of a comfortable spot on my cot, I often wondered what it was like for a whole family to sleep in one room. In *The Children of Sánchez*, Oscar Lewis has recorded his interviews with a family living in the slums of Mexico City. One of the children, a girl like Maela, talks about how she felt sharing a room with her family.

As I grew older, I became more aware of the restrictions one had to put up with when a whole family lived in a single room. In my case, because I lived in fantasy and liked to daydream, I was especially annoyed by having my dreams interrupted. My brothers would bring me back to reality with, "Hey, what's the matter with you! You look dopey!" Or I'd hear my father's voice, "Wake up, you! Always in the clouds! Get moving, fast!"

Coming back to earth, I had to forget the pretty home I was imagining and I looked at our room with more critical eyes. The crude dark wardrobe, so narrow it reminded me of a coffin, was crowded with the clothing of five, seven, or nine people, depending on how many were living there at the time. . . . Dressing and undressing without being seen was a problem. At night we had to wait until the light was out or undress under the blanket, or go to sleep in our clothing. . . .

It would have been a great luxury to be able to linger at the mirror to fix my hair or put on my make-up; I never could because of the sarcasm and ridicule of those in the room. . . . To this day, I look in the mirror hastily, as though I were doing something wrong. I also had to put up with the remarks when I wanted to sing, or lie in a certain comfortable position or do anything that was not acceptable to my family.

Living in one room one must go at the same rhythm as the others, willing or unwillingly. . . . For example, we all had to go to bed at the same time, when my father told us to. Even when we were grown up, he would say, "To bed! Tomorrow is a work day!" This might be as early as eight or nine o'clock, when we weren't all that sleepy. . . . Many times I wanted to draw or read in the evening, but no sooner did I get started when "To bed! Lights out!" and I was left with my drawing in my head or the story unfinished.

A MAN'S LIFE

For Mingo, life on that insecure barricade between subsistence and starvation was no easier than for Paula. He had had dreams when he first came to Juárez. He wanted a job with pay. But he couldn't get a permit to work in El Paso, and he didn't want to leave his family for the long wandering harvest season with the *braceros*, the Mexican migrant laborers who used to work the fields of the United States. After Mingo lost his job at the ice factory he could get only occasional day jobs at the slaughterhouse. There were no other jobs to be had.

Juárez was brimming over with men and women who had come north looking for work. The few factories, the city hall, and the tourist facilities did not provide labor for all of them. Each person was easily vulnerable to losing whatever job he found because so many people were waiting to take his place. Employers paid only the lowest wages and didn't have to correct dangerous, unsanitary working conditions.

The drinking years were probably not too pleasant for Mingo either. The escape into fantasy had to end each night with the sight of his hungry, reproachful wife and children.

Now he spent the whole day in his tiny woodworking business. He'd pick up forty cents' worth of lumber at the yard, then borrow his brother's tools, walking a mile to the colonia López Mateos to pick them up. After several hours he'd turned the lumber into a simple ironing board, and he and Pepe would deliver it to a customer or peddle it door-to-door. The day's work profited him about a dollar.

During those long evenings when he hugged Teresita on his lap, when he talked in his slow, quiet way he never said how he felt about the way life had worked out for him. But he'd often stare off into the distance, his mind some place far away from that plain wooden table.

A SICK LITTLE GIRL

One morning Socorro didn't want to get up. Her stomach ached and she had to vomit. As the day went on, she threw up continuously, her forehead got hotter and hotter, and her stomach felt hard as a knot. She lay in the big bed, her eyes staring up, dark and round.

Her illness terrified us all. She wasn't getting any better, but there was no money for a doctor. Paula coaxed her to eat every kind of food she could think of, but it wouldn't stay down. After two days she went to an old woman who cured illness with special herbs and prayers. But her teas would not stay in Socorro's dehydrated little body; her prayers didn't work for the small child. The next day Don Rafael Castillo, their highly respected neighbor, arrived with a friend who had once been an army medic. He was carrying a jar filled with glucose solution.

It was nighttime. I held the flashlight while the ex-medic went to work. He pounded a nail into the rafter over Socorro's bed, then suspended the jar from it with a length of string. He stuck the needle into a tiny vein on the back of her hand. Her face winced as the needle went in. He taped it down, but a slight hand movement dislodged it. He tried over and over until he finally secured it. At last the fluid began to drip slowly into her vein. Her small face peered solemnly up at us. She didn't dare to move for fear of disconnecting the needle again.

For the next two hours the adults sat around the bed talking quietly; the children were silent. Mingo, Paula, Don Rafael, and the ex-medic complained bitterly about the Mexican government.

"They do nothing for us poor people. They don't care about us. It's their fault if Socorro dies," Paula said. She rarely talked about politics, but now she was angry.

"It's not just government," said Don Rafael. "It's the rich people too. They have money for doctors. They have power; they can bribe politicians and bureaucrats. They don't want to pay taxes, so they twist the government away from us. They were the enemies our fathers fought in the Revolution, and they're our enemies now."

As the liquid slowly dripped into her blood, Socorro's eyes began to shine again. She giggled at one of Maela's jokes and asked for a drink of water. Suddenly, the mood in the room changed. Paula served coffee and sweet rolls, and we began to laugh. Socorro would live. The next day she ate some soup. A few days later she was back in school.

A QUICK GLANCE AT MEXICAN HISTORY

The Revolution that Don Rafael was talking about was not the first bloody war waged in Mexico. Before the white man came to America, the Aztec army ruled a vast empire of conquered tribes and nations. Then Cortés landed at Veracruz in 1519 to conquer the land for Spain, send its gold back to the royal treasury, and convert its people to the holy Roman Catholic Church. His conquest cost thousands of Aztec lives. He captured the emperor and laid siege to the beautiful city of Tenochtitlán. Finally so many had died of hunger and disease that Cortés took the city.

The Mexican War for Independence from Spain lasted over

seven years. *The Independentistas* won in 1821. The new government served the interests of the white Mexicans but did very little for the vast majority, the Indians. The government became a corrupt feudal dictatorship.

When the first Anglo settlers from the United States moved into Texas, the land was a Mexican province, ruled by an autocratic governor. The newcomers wanted the right to own slaves, which the Constitution of independent Mexico forbade. They also resented having to take orders from the government in Mexico City. In 1835 these new settlers revolted against Mexico. After their famous rout at the Alamo in San Antonio, they regrouped their forces and drove the Mexican army out of the province. They proclaimed themselves an independent republic. The Mexicans never recognized the Texans' legal right to the territory, but they couldn't do anything about it.

Ten years later, the United States annexed Texas, which they knew would provoke Mexico into war. Many North Americans, like Congressman Abraham Lincoln, opposed the war. He called it a greedy, imperialistic venture. Before it was over, U.S. forces had captured Mexico City. The victorious army annexed almost half of Mexico, territory which Mexico had long refused to sell them. This is how the states of California, New Mexico, Arizona, Utah, and parts of Colorado became part of the United States.

Mexico continued as an underdeveloped feudal country, ruled by a dictator who cared only for the interests of the wealthy landowners of Spanish descent. The Indians had no rights but lived as serfs, as pieces of human property. They had no protection when the landowners seized more and more of their fields. For the Indians there were no schools, hospitals, or universities. For the landowners there were mansions, luxurious banquets, race tracks, trips to Europe, and universities.

The Mexican Revolution was fought to change those conditions. From 1910 to 1917, peasant guerrillas fought the Federal

Army throughout the country. Hundreds of thousands of people, soldiers and civilians, died. The new government that came to power was dedicated to improving the standard of living for the Indians and rural peasants. It redistributed the lands of the enormous *haciendas* among the peasants who had worked them. It built schools and sent teachers out into the countryside. The new government laid railroad tracks, built highways, nationalized the oil wells, and invested in new mines and factories. It also encouraged private corporations to develop new industries and left them to operate freely.

The Constitution of 1917 changed the whole political system in Mexico. There is now only one official political party, the Institutional Revolutionary Party—or P.R.I. Candidates for the elections, which are held every six years, are chosen from within the party. A few opposition parties exist, but none of their candidates has ever succeeded in reaching high office. Since 1917 there have been regular elections and no coups or military interventions.

Despite its political stability, Mexico has not succeeded in creating an economic development program to rid the country of its terrible poverty. True, there are new factories, new industries, tourist attractions, and a growing middle class. The men who own the factories, the banks, and the large ranches still have great influence over the government's political and economic decisions. The effect of these decisions is to increase the profits of large industries and make the upper classes wealthier. The poorer half of the population continues to live in one-room houses, eating beans and tortillas and worrying about their sick children and their next day's food.

NORTH OF THE BORDER

$\mathcal{T}$he United States still exerts a great deal of influence on
Mexican affairs. It was easy to see that in Juárez. For millions of Mexico's poor, the United States is the promised land.
Once a Mexican safely (and illegally) gets past the U.S. Border
Patrol, he can usually find work. His wages will be low, his
hours long. He'll work under difficult, sometimes dangerous,
conditions. Always he lives in fear—a friend, an enemy, a
stranger, or an employer may report him to the border patrol.
And his own family life is completely disrupted. But the money
he can send home makes it all worth the hardship. That income
will go to enlarge the house, feed the children better, maybe to
buy a little more land, a car, or to start a small business.

Such an arrangement benefits both the Mexican economy and
the businesses in the United States that exploit this cheap, de-
fenseless labor. The workers pour millions of dollars into the
Mexican economy without any investment by the Mexican
government.

Poverty also makes it attractive for U.S. corporations like
RCA to build plants in Mexico, where they can get a lot of work
done for very low wages. The United States is a big market
for Mexico's inexpensive products, while Mexico imports millions of dollars worth of expensive U.S. goods.

An afternoon shopping trip into El Paso with Paula showed
us in microcosm the economic relationship of Mexico to the
United States. We took the orange bus down to the crowded
plaza, then walked through the heart of tourist Juárez toward
the border bridges. The fact that Paul and I were with Paula
made no difference to the men who earn their livings off rich
gringo tourists. Our tall white bodies were the magnet. "Meester,

you wanna buy a lovlee picture?" "Taxi, meessus?" "Step een here please, I have just the theeng for you!"

These men seemed like clinging caricatures, escapees from our worst cartoons. We couldn't avoid them. Paula was embarrassed too, she'd never had to pay attention to them before. Finally we reached the bridge. Down below, a cluster of boys standing on the river bank shouted up, "One penny, meester?" They were waiting to dive for the coins which tourists threw over the bridge.

At the United States end of the bridge it was our turn to feel embarrassed. As tourists, obviously from the States, we had no trouble at either end, but Paula had to show the border patrolman many different papers. Although she was not allowed to earn money in El Paso, she had a visa which permitted her unlimited entries to spend her money shopping there. After her visa was stamped and her shopping bag searched, we went on.

A couple of blocks from the bridge, past rows of rundown apartment buildings, we turned onto a broad street lined with large stores like Newberry's, Woolworth's, and Aaronson's. For Paula, Woolworth's was a world of endless possibilities. Its aisles of merchandise tantalized her with so many beautiful things for her adobe home. Shopping there was easy because everything was labeled in Spanish, the clerks spoke Spanish, and they took pesos as well as dollars.

Paula hurried past the plastic flowers, the religious tapestries, the plastic cups, and the toys. She had money only for fabric. We headed straight for the remnant table, where she examined every piece of cloth. By careful cutting and sewing she could make two dresses out of an eighty-cent remnant. The print was a little fuzzy, but the dresses would fit well, and they would always be clean and pressed.

On our way back we stopped at a stand just in front of the bridge to buy eggs and lard. They were several cents cheaper there than in Juárez. Paul and I bought each child a candy bar.

A MEXICAN WHO DIED IN OUR WAR

The Martínezes had neighbors whose daughter was engaged to a soldier in Vietnam. The family was much better off than the Martínezes because their brother worked as a horse trainer in Los Angeles. With the money he sent them, they had cemented their floors, installed plumbing, and bought a modern kitchen. They often invited us over to visit. The father taught Paul some words of the Indian language he had grown up speaking.

Their daughter's fiancé joined the U.S. Army because he knew it would be easier to get his citizenship papers that way. He had improved his English greatly and expected to find a job in El Paso when he was discharged. The daughter had also worked in El Paso as a maid, but she'd had to sneak across the border to get to work. Together they had banked their earnings so they could buy a house. They wanted to raise their children in El Paso, for the schools were better there, and opportunities existed for them that they'd never find in Mexico. The army had sent him to Vietnam. The family used to ask us where it was, and why we were fighting there.

One morning she got a telegram. He was killed—the first Mexican national to die in Vietnam. We didn't know what to say to her. Clothed in black, she wept in her parents' living room, stroking the doll he had sent her from Hawaii.

DON RAFAEL CASTILLO

Most of Mingo's neighbors had worked in the States, or had relatives there. Don Rafael Castillo had been a bracero for many years. He was very curious to know what two gringos were doing in his colonia; he didn't believe what we told him. No university in the United States, he said, with all its professors, would send students to the colonia la Zapata to learn Spanish. No, he thought, we must be CIA agents, or Protestant missionaries, or scouts for the border patrol.

He was right to be suspicious, for our trainers had not been honest with the Mexicans in arranging for us to live in Juárez. They knew that the Mexican government had rejected a United States offer to send Peace Corps volunteers to work in Mexico. The Mexicans felt no need for them, but our trainers thought the Mexicans were just stubbornly proud. They were afraid the mayor would deny us permission to live in Juárez, so they told him that we were students who wanted to practice our Spanish and learn about Mexican culture.

I'm sure that Don Rafael wouldn't have minded our being Peace Corps trainees. He would have enjoyed teaching us. When the mayor finally discovered what we were doing there, he didn't mind. Hiding our identity did affect me and Paul though. It reinforced our fears that there really was something surreptitious about our role, something to be ashamed of. Maybe we were secret agents of our government after all.

At our first meeting, Don Rafael looked us over carefully as he sat drinking coffee in Paula's living room. It had occurred to him that we might teach English to his son Chencho. He wasn't sure, though, for our mispronounced, poorly constructed Spanish made him think that we were stupid. He spoke slowly and loudly as he invited us to visit him.

The next afternoon he was waiting for us, sitting back in a wooden chair under a tree by his kitchen door. His son brought out two chairs for us. Don Rafael sent his small grandson to the *tienda*, or store, to bring us sodas. He asked us in slow, careful Spanish how we liked the colonia. His eyes laughed at us as he talked. He was wearing a western hat, a faded gray shirt and pants, and old boots. His body was lean and strong, but he sat back wearily in the chair, worn from long years of work. He listened patiently as we struggled to make ourselves understood. Wryly he would ask Paul if he understood what he was saying. "*¿ Sabe Ud. que quiere decir Diós, Pablo?*" ("Do you know what God means, Paul?") he asked, launching into a discussion of whether the Jews still bore the responsibility for the death of Christ. He had learned in Sunday school that they were the Christ killers, and he was astonished to find a live Jew, Paul, sitting in his yard. Finally he decided that perhaps Paul himself was not responsible, but he refused to believe that the pope had absolved all the Jews.

Soon Chencho came over, and Don Rafael asked me to teach him some English. He was twenty-one and lived in one room of Don Rafael's house with his wife and baby. I soon discovered that English is hard to teach, especially since Chencho was much less interested in learning it than his father. He was a cheerful guy, who loved to drive around in his old car. He invited us to come for a ride to the country the next day and went off to find his wife.

Don Rafael must have decided that our motives were not harmful. He invited us to drop by anytime. We were an eager audience for his stories, and we wanted to know his opinions on most things; he liked that.

He was the patriarch of a large family, and the owner of one of the biggest houses in the colonia. He and his wife, Doña Juana, lived in a room with a double bed and a wardrobe off the kitchen. Next to their room, but opening onto the yard was Chencho's, and then came Filiberto's, the bachelor son. Doña Juana ran the household, relying on her daughter-in-law for help. She was a short, round woman. Despite the years of cooking, washing, and worrying she was a cheerful person, though it took time to get past her shy manner. She spoke slowly and quietly.

She was always working when we were there. I picture her now in a faded blue, flower-print dress, the sleeves rolled up, her hair pulled back in a bun, standing over a tin washtub, scrubbing clothes on the washboard.

Manuel, the oldest son, was financially successful. He earned about fifty dollars a week driving a truck in El Paso. He and his wife lived next door with their four children in a house he had built. Their house was quite modern. His wife used a wringer washing machine for the laundry and cooked on a gas stove. They had a refrigerator and a large television set.

Don Rafael rarely visited Manuel's house, but Chencho did a lot of lounging on the couch in front of the TV. Television was a window into the United States. The family watched cartoons, movies, and commercials in English and Spanish. One afternoon we were all watching a rock and roll show from Los Angeles when Chencho said, "Those black singers are ugly. Would you let your daughter marry one?"

"Of course, why not?" I replied.

"You're crazy. They're animals. It's always the blacks who get arrested downtown."

Chencho's prejudice shocked us. Had it come from TV? Probably some of it did, but some was the reaction of an unsophisticated boy to a different physical type. I learned quickly that prejudice is not confined simply to the United States.

TV suggested to Chencho the dimensions of a life beyond the colonia. It contributed to his restlessness, made him dream of adventure. He loved and respected his father; he would always live at home. But he didn't want to work like a slave, as Don Rafael had for so many years. For the moment he took out his restlessness by speeding along the highway outside of Juárez.

Sitting back under the shade of his tree was a new pleasure for Don Rafael. Until his sons were old enough to help support him, he had been a bracero. He too had come to Juárez from a small southern village, another refugee from the poverty of the farm. But instead of settling for a local job, Don Rafael left his wife and sons to travel north across the border. Over the face of the United States he had gone—picking crops, laying tracks, digging ditches. Those had been years of long back-breaking hours at work, of shabby, overcrowded bunkhouses, of paltry, starchy meals. Amid the hardship and loneliness he had found adventure and companionship. When the season was over each year he came back with dollars in his pocket. That money had built his house, fed his family, and educated his children.

In some ways, he says, the United States was good to him. But it also treated him badly. Paul and I reminded him of the people who had treated him like an ignorant "spic." His experiences had left him proud and angry.

One night we were talking about the braceros, and about the law which the U.S. Congress had just passed barring Mexicans from getting temporary visas to work during the harvests. Don Rafael said, "We are just the Mexican poor. Your government doesn't want us any more. I know how to read and write. That was all that mattered then. Now you make us fill out all those application papers. Then you never accept us anyway.

"I want you to know how much I love America," he went on. "I lived there and would never say evil things about it. But I never had a single gringo friend. People there think we Mexicans are no better than beasts. In small towns, when I was traveling, I would knock on doors, hoping to trade a few hours' work for a meal and a place to sleep. I can't tell you how many people called the police when they saw me. I was only a "Mex," a "spic."

Until then, I had supported the bracero law as a humanitarian measure to end the exploitation of Mexican workers and to keep ranchers from using imported scab labor to break strikes called by union organizers of farm workers. Now here was Don Rafael telling me that it was a racist law. Surely there was a way that the United States could let people like Don Rafael work without exploiting them. We are the richest country in the world.

Don Rafael was enjoying his hard-earned retirement. "Helping my people is my job now," he said. "Just like I helped Socorro when she was sick." He was always sitting out in his yard, chatting with someone, keeping his sharp eyes on the road. Keeping tabs on the colonia.

He didn't talk politics that much when we were around. But one afternoon he, Paula, Mingo, and another neighbor started complaining about rising food prices. They were angry at their government, bitter about the poverty which they knew they worked too hard to deserve. Bred to despair, they dreaded that the only change in their lives would be for the worse. They had heard too many campaigning politicians invoke memories of the Revolution as they made extravagant promises, then watched while the politicians got rich and the people stayed poor. Corn and milk prices kept rising. Even beans were beginning to get expensive.

BARBED WIRE

Time passed quickly. We wanted to spend as much time as we could in the colonia with the Martínezes, with Don Rafael, and with the dozens of other people who welcomed us into their homes. We resented the hours spent in class—they were as boring and irrelevant as ever.

We also wanted to learn more about another important aspect of life in the colonia—the U.S. Border Patrol. Disobeying our trainers, who said that the border patrol was irrelevant to our training and that El Paso was off limits, we made an appointment to visit the El Paso Detention Facility, run by the U.S. Department of Justice.

A friend of Mingo's, who had been locked up there for several days once, said that it was as hot as an oven there. "The food had no taste, and they crowded us into rooms that were so hot it was hard to breathe."

An officer who showed us around looked at it differently. "These beds are more comfortable than any these people have ever slept on," he said, "and the food is very nutritious. At Thanksgiving last year, we even gave them a turkey dinner."

Behind the tall chain-link fences topped with rolls of barbed wire, groups of men leaned against the wall of the buildings, hugging to the narrow band of shade. Heat waves rising from the flat dirt yard blurred the image. In response to some barked orders they formed into a long line and shambled to the mess hall.

Our guide was a young patrolman who loved his job. He showed us a display of weapons various agents had taken from armed aliens and nodded briefly toward a plaque on the wall that recorded the names of those officers killed in the line of duty.

I was surprised at how sympathetic he was to the plight of most of the people he is paid to apprehend. "Most of them are poor men, with tremendous energy and courage, who are just trying to make a living for their families. I'd probably do the same thing if I was in their place. But I've got a job to do and it has its rewards. I love to catch a criminal, and anyway I'm being paid to do what I like best—go hunting. Only hunting people is more challenging, because they're smarter than animals."

Standing in that room, I was right on the line between my country and my new friends. The vague assumption that my country's borders were legitimate lines to be defended was suddenly jolted. A picture flashed through my mind: I saw this genial man turn his flashlight on Mingo and Pepe, grab them, and lock them into that dingy oven of a camp. He was forcing them out of the richest nation in the world.

Continuing my dramatic fantasy, I linked arms with Mingo and stood up to that man in his green uniform and his wide-brimmed hat. We challenged the United States to throw open its doors and share its wealth.

FAREWELL

The month was over. We had to go back to Albuquerque. With tears, embraces, and promises to write we left the Martínezes and boarded the Bluebird.

We had one more week of training. We all spent the last day nervously waiting for the director to hand out those envelopes which would tell if we had been accepted or "deselected." Our acceptance was immediately qualified: Paul and I had been put on "administrative hold." We might not pass the security check. The FBI had described our antiwar group in Chicago as a chapter of Students for a Democratic Society in Paul's file, and listed him as chairman. They were wrong on both counts, but we had to wait for ten more days while they looked further into our backgrounds. Finally the FBI decided that none of us was sufficiently subversive to warrant dismissal.

We were finally excited about starting our life in Ecuador. June 9, 1966, at 11:00 P.M., the twenty remaining members of our group boarded a Braniff jet for Guayaquil.

4

Working in Ecuador

DOWNTOWN GUAYAQUIL

The jet was bright turquoise, Braniff Airline's gimmick to attract passengers. The stewardess wrinkled her nose when I told her we were going to Guayaquil. "I've never wanted to get off there," she said. "It's so hot, and it smells strange."

Guayaquil was immediately, obviously different from any place I had ever lived. The sticky heat of its tropical rainy season left the sweat clinging to my body like damp long underwear. Odors hung densely in the air—I'd walk from the perfume of a hibiscus hedge into the acrid stench of urine baking on the rutted cement sidewalk. The variety was sometimes overwhelming: frying meats, roasting bananas, leaky sewer pipes, overflowing trash cans, and piles of cocoa beans drying rich and chocolaty on the sidewalk.

Downtown Guayaquil was a twenty-block area, which in 1966 contained only a few tall concrete business and apartment buildings. It had one department store—which featured an up escalator—a couple of supermarkets, one or two elegant shops, several attractive hotels. The most handsome building was the new Social Security Office, decorated with a colorful mural, and the most ornate was the Italian-baroque-styled city hall. The area fronts on the Malecón, a boulevard along the wide, muddy brown Guayas River. I used to love to sit below the statue of Simón Bolívar and watch the river life. Flat rafts of balsa logs, dugout canoes, discarded World War II barges, and wooden motor launches contrasted with the large foreign freighters anchored in the middle of the river.

The streets going back from the river were lined with three-story wooden or brick buildings. They jutted over the sidewalks to form an arcade sheltering pedestrians from the tropical rains and the afternoon sun. Their tired façades, with their rusting metal work and their worn paint, hinted at a more elegant past and masked the crowded tenements they had become. In many of the one-room houses a whole family lived; there was one water spigot and one toilet to a building. Small shops, opening off the sidewalk arcades, occupied the ground floors, each shop crowded with one kind of merchandise—tin washtubs and pots, or fabrics and notions, or second-hand sewing machines and old irons, or groceries, or prescriptions.

Except during siesta, when the heat made most activity un-bearable, the sidewalks were crowded from early morning until late at night. Men sat together around small sidewalk cafe tables, drinking a morning coffee or an afternoon beer, talking ani-matedly, laughing, and competing to fashion the most flowery compliment for passing women. Wearing high heels, fitted dresses, and carefully arranged hairdos, the women hurried to finish their shopping, often tugging small children along, fre-quently stopping to embrace a friend and exchange the latest family news.

Adding to the noise and the commotion were the street vendors —everywhere men, women, and children hawking almost every-thing in an insistent singsong. "Hard-boiled eggs, get your fresh little hard-boiled eggs," called women carrying large baskets.

"Pork sandwiches! I've got delicious pork sandwiches," cried out men standing beside their wooden carts.

One peddler even sold plastic earrings shaped like the little bones worn by the Flintstones on TV.

"¡Cigarillos, cigarillos!" The high cry would come insistently closer until a thin arm waved a pack of contraband Winstons in front of my nose. The boy would follow me for blocks, refusing to believe that I didn't want his cigarettes.

A father and son, each carrying a box of flowering plants on his head, one high and one low, threaded their way through the crowd.

The beggars almost outnumbered the hawkers; the afflictions they were parading were almost as varied as the peddlers' merchandise. A small thin girl brought her blind grandfather downtown almost every day and led him from table to table at the sidewalk cafes as she whined for a donation. A young man without arms walked about with lottery tickets pinned to his sleeveless shirt, pleading with people to buy. A boy whose legs were horribly twisted by polio sat on a little wagon stretching his arms up for a donation. Shoeshine boys swept through the cafes in small gangs. They sat down at our feet and refused to leave until we had given them a nickel to dust off our shoes.

At first Paul and I would leave a cafe when a beggar approached. It was unbearable to deal with that army of the maimed and the grotesque. We couldn't give money to them all; we couldn't let each one shine our shoes. It was impossible to concentrate on a conversation with their mournful eyes gazing at us. Defensively we'd start to hate them, then we developed the emotional calluses which had shocked us in other volunteers. We learned to ignore them.

THE BARRIOS

It took time for Paul and me to establish roots in Guayaquil. We spent our first month living in a small downtown hotel with the other volunteers while we all looked for a place to live and for jobs to do. The men played pinochle for hours. They developed a language of private jokes and metaphors to defend themselves against the confusing pain of moving out into a strange environment. At the hotel we met volunteers who'd been in Ecuador for months. But only a few of them talked with warmth or excitement about the communities in which they were living or about their work. Most spoke depreciatingly about the Ecuadorians, the "Ekkies." Most were disillusioned with the Peace Corps.

We would set out each morning from the hotel to look for a house in the *barrios suburbanos*, or suburban districts. Our project director in Guayaquil was a social worker from Chicago who chomped a big cigar and talked to us as though he were addressing a person standing ten feet away from us and who often responded to urgent questions in vague generalities. (When I had imagined being a Peace Corps volunteer overseas I never thought I'd be responsible to a boss from the United States— it would be just me and the people of that country. It turned out otherwise.) He hung a map of the city and its outlying barrios on his wall and stuck a pin flagged with each of our names on the spot where we chose to live. He was a general deploying his troops strategically throughout the *suburbios*. We were to begin organizing a federation of community organizations, giving the poor from all geographical parts of the barrios a voice in their government.

The barrios suburbanos are communities built up out of the

saltwater swamps that ring the downtown area. As peasants moved to the city in search of a better life, they formed groups to invade unoccupied land, just as Mingo and Paula had done. Only this land was so wet that they built their houses on stilts. They walled the rooms with split bamboo poles and roofed them with sheets of corrugated zinc. They tied wires into the nearest electric lines, and built bamboo walkways back to solid ground. Gradually, the ground around the houses was filled and the spaces between the rows of houses became roads. In the summer, these treeless roads were dusty; in the winter they became muddy, flooded ditches.

A small barrio called Isla San José was typical of the poorer barrios that grew up along the banks of the saltwater estuaries that laced the great swamp. Some fishermen had erected their bamboo shanties and then petitioned the city to fill in the muddy water beneath them. Finally, after years of empty promises from the municipio, they persuaded the sanitation department to dump the garbage into the water. When we first visited Isla San José, the city had already filled in more than an acre with garbage.

That day we arrived just as a garbage truck was backing out of a short street. Its load lay freshly dumped at the water's edge. Digging, poking, and prying, dozens of people combed through the heap. Flies hovered all around them in a giant buzzing cloud. A woman pulled out a doll whose left arm was missing and gave it to her daughter. Behind us we heard a tinny, grating noise. We turned around quickly to see six vultures swooping down onto a patched zinc roof. Their hooded eyes darted eagerly over the scene, their bare necks craning in the search for rat carcasses. Just then a small boy hurtled around the corner, pushing an empty rusted oil drum with a stick and laughing. His naked bronzed belly was bloated, but his rib cage poked out against the taut skin of his chest, each bone clearly outlined.

After days of trudging along dusty roads past gray bamboo shacks and occasional crooked brick houses, a house appeared as though a mirage. It was yellow stucco with a red-tiled roof, and was surrounded by a garden and a high wall. A "For Rent" sign hung on the gate, and inside it had plumbing, running water, and more rooms than we could use. The rent was thirty dollars a month. With our Peace Corps allowance we bought a noisy blue fifth-hand refrigerator, and a two-burner hotplate, a bed, a table, and chairs.

Having our own place restored our privacy and removed us from the bickering company of the other volunteers. Once settled in our new house, though, we unexpectedly began to feel isolated. We were strangers. When we got on a bus to ride into town, the other passengers would laugh when Paul bumped his head on the roof, banged his knees on the seat, and squished into a place that was designed for smaller people. We looked different, we dressed differently, and we lived in the big house. People were polite, often friendly, but they treated us like foreigners.

I had long ago given up my image of Peace Corps people living in grass huts, but I was surprised to find myself living so comfortably. Our living allowance, $100 a month apiece, put us firmly in the middle-class income bracket. The goods we'd brought from home—a large fan, an electric frying pan, and a typewriter—made us rich by the standards of our neighbors in the barrio. The disparity made me uncomfortable; I felt both guilty and self-conscious.

When I went to the store to buy food for breakfast, I'd get four eggs, four rolls, two bananas, and instant coffee. Most families had only coffee and rolls. Everybody could see that we woke up later than they because the night light was often burning over our front door at 8:00 A.M., wasting pennies' worth of electricity. The two of us shared five rooms, while at least six Ecuadorians lived in each one-room house on the block.

If Paul forgot to take the bottles back the morning after he bought beer, the owner of the tienda would send his son to collect them, for the bottles were more valuable than the beer.

Our neighbors bought one cigarette at a time, while Paul bought them by the pack. Everybody burned their trash in the dirt road out front, but we were the only people who ever threw out food. Each night somebody would sift through our garbage for leftovers.

People would stop us on the street to ask if they could buy our clothes when we were finished with them. They asked me to hire them to clean my house, do my washing, sew my clothes; they wanted me to help them get a passport to the States or to recommend them for a job with other North Americans.

It astonished them that we would be living in their barrio. Certainly upper-class Guayaquileños wouldn't dream of living out there. To them the people of the barrios were both an ignorant breed who should be treated like children and a potentially dangerous group from whom one needed police protection.

Our neighbors would ask us politely, "*¿Y qué es su misión aquí?*" ("And what is your mission here?") They told one another that we were either CIA agents or Protestant missionaries, Jehovah's Witnesses most likely. Why else would anyone from such a rich country as the United States be living in the barrios suburbanos? It was months before I got to know anyone well enough so that they related to me as Raquel Cowan, individual human being, rather than as *la rubia*, "the blonde," or the curious gringa.

SOME FACTS ABOUT ECUADOR

Ecuador is divided into three geographical regions: the Pacific coast, the Sierra (high Andes mountain range), and the Amazonian rain forest. Though the Equator cuts through the country (hence its name), its climate ranges from steamy tropical

73

heat in the lowlands to subzero winds on the snow-covered volcanic peaks of the Andes.

The population of six million is divided into equally distinct racial groups, with the Indians of the Andes living in a culture that is still remote from that of the whites and mestizos of the coast. Most Ecuadorians are Indians, nearly all of them descended from the citizens of the Inca Empire. Only the Indians of the Amazon forest escaped the powerful Inca army, just as they continue to avoid contact with Ecuador's contemporary government. (As oil companies push further into the wilderness, however, the Indians are faced with extinction.) The majority of Indians still speak Quechua, rather than Spanish, and view the whites and mestizos as completely untrustworthy. Ever since the Spanish conquistadors came to Ecuador in the 1500s, the Indians have been oppressed. Landowners have paid them virtually nothing for doing all the work on their properties. Until recently the Indians have had no schools, and they cannot vote unless they learn Spanish.

The next largest segment of the population are the mestizos, part Spanish and part Indian. When an Indian learns Spanish, cuts his braid, adopts the European style of dress, and wears shoes, he can become a mestizo. Most mestizos, though, do have some Spanish blood and live on the coast. There are also blacks in Ecuador whose ancestors escaped from wrecked slave ships. At the top of the social order are the small group of pure whites, whose ancestors came from Spain or other parts of Europe.

Racial and cultural differences are exploited by Ecuador's ruling elite to maintain a constant state of political instability. The merchants of the coast fight the rich landowners of the Sierra for the power to decide how the national income will be collected and spent. The people of the coast want roads, ports, and factories built down there, while the upper class in Quito wants money to go for the development of roads and agriculture in the Sierra. Neither of them is concerned about spending money to serve the needs of the working and lower classes. The poor and the wealthy of the coast unite in hating the *serranos*, or mountain people, while the poor and the wealthy in the Sierra despise the *costeños*, or coastal people. Historically, one junta has overthrown a popularly elected president, then another coup has installed a new group of governors, then another, followed by another election, and so on.

Although nearly all Ecuadorians are Catholics, the Church has always been loyal to its wealthy parishioners, not to its poor. It has run most upper-class schools, and it owns large haciendas worked by serfs. Its bishops come from the upper class. The Church has prospered on the profits from its haciendas and on money collected from the poor as well as the rich. In return, the poor have been counselled to suffer patiently until the next life. Those dedicated priests who have tried to help organize peasants to demand their rights have been punished, not encouraged. Ecuadorian priests get transferred when they become outspoken, foreign priests are expelled. Nevertheless, a movement of radical priests is growing—they feel they have to work against the Church Establishment.

Ecuador is an underdeveloped country that has not tapped many of its natural resources nor realized its agricultural potential. It could produce more sugar, more meat, more rice, more coffee, more oil—and more important it could keep more of the revenues from the export of these materials if it controlled them. Instead, the government allows most of the profits to be sent to banks in the States, and has done little to create the jobs from which Ecuadorians could earn enough to pay for adequate food, clothing, and shelter.

CULTURE SHOCK

Back in Albuquerque the trainers had impressed on us that we would find Ecuador a poor country. They had even shown us slides of the bamboo houses in the barrios. But they didn't prepare me for the emotional effect of seeing that much desperate poverty. I felt dizzy and nauseated from the impact of so many images: the beggars, the rickety shacks above the putrid swamps, the hysterical wails of a mother following her baby's tiny white coffin to the cemetery.

It took a long time for me to see past the bleak imagery. I didn't like Guayaquil or the people I was meeting nearly as much as I'd liked Juárez. The people seemed so beaten down; they had little faith in themselves or their country. The children in our barrio seemed to play more destructive, less creative games than the children in Juárez. They were always throwing rocks, playing hitting games with sticks. People's conversations seemed superficial.

We grew more and more depressed. We missed our family, our old friends, our familiar places, and current books and magazines. Our moods fluctuated wildly. Some days we'd be elated because we'd learned something important, or met somebody nice, or talked to someone who wanted us to work with him. Other days we'd feel so down we could barely manage to leave the house and face all those people who didn't really care whether we existed and who spoke a language it took all our energy to understand.

We had all the symptoms of culture shock. The Peace Corps had warned us that many volunteers' marriages break up under the strain. Couples either help each other through the hard times, or they take out their frustrations on each other. We did have tensions. Sometimes I would cry from feeling so lonely, and I'd feel worse when Paul couldn't make the hurting go away. He in turn would feel that I didn't support him strongly enough in the fights he had decided to have with our Peace Corps directors.

He correctly perceived that our problem was not simply culture shock. We were the victims of poor planning by the Peace Corps. We had been brought to a city which we'd been led to believe both needed and wanted us. But only one or two city hall bureaucrats even cared if we showed up for work, and very few volunteers found ready acceptance in their barrios. Paul saw right away that there was very little useful work we could do in Guayaquil—so far the Peace Corps had been there for five years with almost nothing to show for all those hours and hours of work. He wanted them to reexamine their thinking, to change their ways of working, and to include volunteers and Ecuadorians in the planning of future projects.

Even though I knew that Paul was right, I hated the fights we were already getting into. Within two months we had a reputation as troublemakers, which made me uncomfortable. I would rather ignore the other volunteers and the directors. I wanted to focus on community projects, both because I found them more interesting than Paul did (partly because my Spanish was a lot better) and because I liked the feeling of being busy, whether or not any great purpose was being accomplished.

As time went on, though, our paths came together. He got more involved in projects, and I became more of an activist in the small group of dissident volunteers that emerged. Our tensions proved to be minor ones. Sharing the Peace Corps experience brought us closer together than we had ever been. We talked about ideas, plans, and books we were reading for long hours. We made new friends, but we became each other's best friend.

OUR BRIEF CAREER IN THE MUNICIPIO

*E*very morning that summer we would leave our house and make the half-hour bus ride to the municipio. We walked through the crowd of people gathered on the plaza outside waiting to see some official or just talking with their friends. Then we took the wire cage elevator to the fourth floor. The high-ceilinged room which was the Office of Community Development was often empty, with the secretary waiting for something to type and another employee waiting for something to do. We pulled chairs up to the table and sat down for our meeting with Jorge Rodríguez, the man who our Peace Corps representative had told us should be replaced. Jorge became one of our closest friends. He was not anti-American, as we had been led to expect. He was just disillusioned with the Peace Corps. The volunteers brought few skills and little long-range commitment. The Peace Corps promised a lot but delivered little.

Jorge welcomed our experience, our ideas, and our trust in him. He wanted us to help him teach courses in community development to students, barrio leaders, and middle-class women. He was ambitious to organize more community centers and to improve the already existing ones. But his office had no funds to expand its programs. As it was, he spent many hours meeting with delegations from community centers who wanted their salaries. Our meetings consisted of 90 percent wishful thinking.

In any case, our career at city hall did not last long. The mayor was forced to resign when he was unable to deal with a strike by the city's sanitation men, and the new mayor did not like Jorge. He wanted to give an abandoned building out in the barrios to a friend who would use it for his business; Jorge wanted to convert it into a community center. When Jorge accepted an invitation to attend a United Nations Seminar on community development in Italy, we were left with a new boss. He didn't want our help, so after two months we quit the very job we had been sent to do. When Jorge came back from Italy, having won first prize in his class, the mayor fired him.

Then we looked around our barrio for a project. Right on our corner there were three different committees working to get street lights installed. They refused to cooperate with one another because their leaders had competing political ambitions. The barrio had no community center or medical clinic, but we were reluctant to start organizing one because we had seen too many other projects which volunteers had initiated and carried through by dint of their own energy, enthusiasm, and connections that had fallen apart when the volunteers left. In the end, we thought, we would be letting people down by organizing them to put such great effort and such amounts of their own meager incomes into a project their government had no commitment to support.

Not having a task, forced to become our own employment agency in a city with very few job openings, we felt extremely marginal to life in Guayaquil. Nevertheless, our depression began to lift. As in Juárez, we began to make friends. Evangelina, one of our neighbors, helped me to break through the barrier of loneliness and prejudice with which I had surrounded myself so that I could see that the people whose lives had at first seemed so depressing and desperate were actually strong individuals with their own joys, sorrows, and rhythms.

EVANGELINA

Evangelina, her husband Julio, and their two small sons, Rolandito and Luis Alfredo, lived in a one-room house built into the corner of the wall around our house. I felt awkward with her at first because I lived in the large house and because she asked to do our laundry. I refused her offer at first, but when I was unable to get any clothes clean with cold water and my knuckles, I agreed.

Evangelina was shyer, daintier, and a little less intense than Paula, but the two women's lives had much in common. Evangelina spent most of her day keeping her family fed, clothed, and clean. She, too, lived with the constant nagging worry that her husband might not come home at night or that he might come home with no pay in his pocket, having squandered it on a drinking binge.

Each morning we woke up when she turned her radio on. A musical commercial for Johnson's Baby Powder blared out as she tuned into the first of the day's *novelas*. Their various plots unfolded through the day as she first washed the dishes in a tin bowl, then scrubbed the clothes in a wooden tub, then ironed on the wooden table, pressing down hard with a charcoal-heated iron, then mopped the morning's accumulation of dust from the board floor, then put the rice and soup on for lunch. Rolando, her four-year-old, was named for the hero of her favorite soap opera.

Evangelina cooked on a charcoal fire, which she kindled in a brick-lined box set in one corner of the house. She had to dip water for cooking, washing, and bathing out of a fifty-gallon oil drum beside the house. Twice a week the water truck stopped outside the gate and filled the drum at a cost of fifteen cents. The family had no toilet; they emptied their chamber pot into the street, just as all their neighbors did.

Ecuadorian food is time-consuming to prepare. Evangelina would have to make several trips a day to the tienda. Mostly she cooked rice, but she served with it various dishes made of boiled, mashed green bananas cooked with onion or little bits of meat. The food tasted fairly bland, but I learned how to make several typical dishes. I showed her how to make tuna-rice casserole and sweet-and-sour pork.

80

Evangelina shared our refrigerator, and in turn she often took me to market with her. Otherwise I would never have dared to negotiate that complicated maze of stalls, each one piled with a fruit or vegetable for which I had to bargain with the vendor. They always doubled their price when they saw my blond hair, so I would then turn and walk away, pretending to have no interest in their wares. They would call me back and offer a lower price. I would hesitate, not wanting to save a penny which they needed more than I did, yet not wanting to be taken advantage of. Evangelina had no doubts about haggling: she stuck with it till the price came down to where she wanted it. When Evangelina wasn't with me, I usually went to a downtown supermarket where the prices were fixed—I just wasn't a good bargainer.

Many afternoons, Evangelina and I would sit on the front steps talking while her children took their naps. She wanted to know if all she'd heard about the fabulous wealth of the United States was true. Did people really throw away their clothes after they'd worn them once? Did every family have two cars? What did the houses look like? Was it easy to get a job?

She told me that she had grown up on a farm in the country, and she hadn't seen her parents for years. I often felt sorry for her as I passed her stooped over the laundry tub. She worked so hard, day after day, and she was so poor.

I stopped pitying her, though, after spending a weekend in September visiting her family back on the farm. She and Julio had saved up for their first visit home since their marriage. The bus fare was two dollars.

COUNTRY COUSINS

Evangelina's home town, San Pablo, was a bumpy eight-hour bus ride away, though it was geographically less than a hundred miles from Guayaquil. For half the trip the road was nothing but two ruts through flat, dusty fields. The land used to be fertile, but a recent seven-year drought had turned it to dust. The small villages scattered over the plain had once been thriving communities where people wove "Panama" hats for a living. Working in the soft light of dawn and dusk so as not to dry out the straw, they bent over their work, straining their eyes. The finest hats took a month to make but earned the weaver only a few dollars. Then when Panama hats went out of style in the United States, the weavers had no way to make a living. Thousands of them left the villages for the barrios of Guayaquil. Their farmer neighbors have recently joined them there, defeated by the persistent drought.

San Pablo is a small town of farmers and fishermen on the shores of a wide bay. The small bamboo houses are built on stilts; the dirt streets below are kept clean by roving pigs. It is a drab but tidy community located between blue waters and green forests.

Evangelina left home when she was a teen-ager because the drought had ruined her father's farm, and he could no longer support the family. She stayed with a cousin in Guayaquil and found work as a seamstress. Her father went to a banana plantation in the Andean foothills while the rest of the family stayed home. But he had hated the life of forced, low-paid labor, and so he had returned to his land. Now he rode his donkey into town every day to bring back barrels of water for his crops and his family. He liked being his own boss.

Until we arrived in San Pablo we had a somewhat romantic image of country life. Once there, though, we were suddenly confronted with the enemy they had warned us about in Peace Corps training. Germs! Parasites! And the deadly chinchorra bug, which bites the mucous membrane while a person sleeps, implanting a parasite that slowly but fatally destroys the heart muscles.

Not that Guayaquil was such a healthy place to live. Germs in the drinking water cause thousands of babies to die of gastro-enteritis, as Socorro almost did. There were rats and rabid dogs, hepatitis germs, and amoebas and parasites in the food. But living in our own house we had figured out how to protect our-selves. In training we had been taught so many precautions that to respect them all was to live behind a plastic barrier between our North American sanitary selves and the germ-infested natives. In Guayaquil we followed as many of the precautions as we could: we boiled all our drinking water, we soaked our lettuce in iodine-tinted water, and we never ate lettuce, tomatoes, or raw-looking meat in restaurants. But as time went on we began to relax—I more than Paul. Since he is a minor hypo-chondriac he continued to take good care of himself, but I ate more recklessly. As a result I got a mild case of hepatitis and often felt nauseated.

But in the country we were guests and we didn't want to offend Evangelina's family. They gave us the best bed, a four poster with a canopy of mosquito netting. The thin mattress lay on bamboo slats, and like all poor Ecuadorians' homes, the house was walled with split bamboo poles. Peace Corps volun-teers are forbidden to live in bamboo houses because they may shelter the chinchorra. Paul and I couldn't refuse the bed, but we slept fitfully.

The next morning we faced a new problem. A pig was dozing in the stream from which the family drew its water. We knew it would be rude to refuse the cup of lemonade which Evan-gelina's aunt offered us at breakfast, but we were afraid of the water. Paul asked if he could have a cup of boiling water in-stead, saying that's what he always drank in the morning. Dis-creetly, I dropped an iodine tablet into my lemonade. The liquid turned black. I quickly covered the glass with my hands and buried it in my lap until I thought the tablet had taken effect. Then I bolted the drink down.

Our visit was a novelty for the villagers, who had never hosted any North Americans. Evangelina's cousins invited us all to lunch and killed a chicken in our honor. While the women prepared a delicious chicken and peanut stew, they listened eagerly as Evangelina described Guayaquil's modern wonders.

"There are tall, tall buildings in the middle of town with elevators that take you up. There is a big store that sells everything you can imagine, and you can ride up to the second floor on a moving staircase. The bus goes right from our corner to the middle of town, and the boys will be able to walk to school. They can learn more in the schools there, and we're going to send them to high school too. There is a hospital and a clinic. People come selling things right to our house, and one of our neighbors has a television set. There's always something to see, something to do."

I had never heard her talk so enthusiastically, with such a lilt in her voice and such a sparkle in her eyes. All of a sudden I saw Guayaquil anew. What appeared to me as the most broken-down slum was a modern metropolis. Evangelina's life in the city was easier, more interesting, and it offered more opportunities. The cousins were envious.

Out on the porch Paul and Julio were sitting with the other men. Julio was talking about Guayaquil's night life, about its lively streets and attractive women. He was earning more on his job than any of them could hope to save from fishing and farming. Later, he took Paul aside and whispered, "These people don't know how to live! They're real hicks!"

MACHISMO

Guayaquil's major sources of employment are the ports, which provide men with jobs as stevedores. That's where

Julio worked, loading hundred-pound stalks of bananas onto freighters. The German company for which he worked paid him twenty dollars a month. He was glad for the steady employment, and his wages were better than most people's in the barrio, but after each ship was loaded, he'd be exhausted for at least a day.

Evangelina supplemented his income with a few sewing jobs, but they had just enough to survive on. An illness, an accident to Julio's back, a robbery, or a blight on the banana harvest would mean no money for food. Ultimately their fortunes depended on a risky, competitive business—banana exporting—where big companies like United Fruit and Standard Fruit are seeking to outsell each other, neither one providing many benefits to their workers. Julio always wished he had his own means of support.

Julio was a handsome, good-natured man who loved his sons and his wife. But he was sometimes unreliable and often demanding. He was the boss. Some paydays he stayed out late, drinking with his *compañeros* from work. Whenever he came home he wanted his meal ready, then he wanted the house quiet so he could sleep, and his white pants and shirt pressed so he could go off to town. Evangelina rarely got to leave the house for a social occasion, except for birthday parties for her relatives.

I admired Evangelina's strength. She was a loyal, supportive wife, a warm and accepting mother, and a tireless worker. When she complained about Julio's behavior, or spoke angrily of the way men treat women in Ecuador, I identified completely with her.

Machismo is the Spanish word for the kind of sexism that dominates male-female relationships in Ecuador and most other countries in Latin America (not to mention many parts of the United States). It is based on the idea that men should be strong, virile, sexually potent, and aggressive, while women must be beautiful, sexy, passive, and obedient. I felt it in most of my relationships with men, and I saw it making life difficult and frustrating for some of my closest women friends.

It was impossible to walk down the street without having men stare at my entire body from head to foot several times over and make loud flowery comments or whistle and smack their lips. It was entirely different but just as annoying to be among a group discussing ideas or projects. There I would feel invisible. The men looked at Paul, listened to Paul, and talked to Paul. They looked startled if I spoke out.

Ecuadorian men regard their wives, daughters, and lovers as their private property. They romanticize them, but do not respect them as equals. Although this machismo sometimes infuriated me, it didn't define me. Sexism was a problem I had long been aware of in my life at home, but machismo did not affect my own self-awareness because I didn't have to live with it permanently. It did restrict Evangelina and her friends. She had to live with the fear of Julio's abandoning her, and she had none of the social freedom that he did.

Her neighbor was worse off. She had to obey her husband and be available whenever he wanted her for anything. If she went off to visit a friend, he would become wildly jealous and beat her. He could have all the love affairs he wanted, but if she even looked at another man her husband would threaten her.

Many men believed that the number of children they had was an indication of their machismo. Not only did it show the world that they were virile, but it also kept the women safely confined to home. They forbade their wives to use any form of birth control.

Julio was not that domineering. He not only loved Evangelina, but he respected her. When she told him that she wanted to go to the family planning clinic, he agreed.

BIRTH CONTROL, SOME VIGNETTES

"Why aren't you pregnant, Raquelita?" Evangelina asked the question with so much embarrassment that I knew she must have been wondering for months. She wasn't the first to ask. Almost every woman I had met in Guayaquil opened our conversation by asking how many children I had. When I said none, they looked apologetic, as if they had just intruded on a private pain. They were too polite to inquire what was wrong.

I told Evangelina that Paul and I wanted to wait until we had finished our work in Ecuador and decided what we wanted to do next. "How do you keep from getting pregnant?" Evangelina asked. "Every month I am terrified that I'll be pregnant again."

I told her about my birth control pills and described the family planning clinic where she could get help. Her shy, gentle face brightened. "I will go there right away. Ever since Luis Alfredo was born I have been praying to God not to send me any more babies. I love the boys but I don't want any more. With Julio's job and my sewing, we can sometimes save a few *sucres* so that maybe we can buy a little piece of land and send the boys to high school. With another child we won't even have enough to eat.

"Besides, you can never really trust a man. Look at Luz América over there, scrubbing all those clothes. Her old man just walked out one day, went to live with another woman. Now she has to take in laundry to feed her five children. I'm not going to let that happen to me!" Evangelina went down to the clinic the following week.

Our conversation persuaded me to volunteer to work in the birth control clinic. There had to be thousands of women like

Evangelina, desperate for that information. The birth control program would be a way to keep families from getting poorer and would give some women a certain amount of control over what happened to their bodies.

The head doctor assigned me to speak to groups in the barrios about family planning. Since many of the women knew nothing about how their bodies actually worked, I drew some big charts of the male and female reproductive systems. When I explained how a baby is conceived and how it is possible to prevent it, many of them gasped. Afterward they crowded around for more information. But only a few, to my disappointment, ever came into the clinic.

After I gave a talk to a class in health and nutrition, one of the mothers came up to me. Her face was already lined, she had lost several teeth, and her body muscles sagged from fatigue. María was not much older than I. "This birth control sounds good," she began. "I have eight children, and my man earns only twenty sucres [one dollar] a day working in the slaughterhouse. We only have two rooms. How can we manage another child? This nutrition class is no help. The teacher tells us to feed our families a balanced diet. With what? Rice and *verdes* [green bananas], that's what we mostly eat. Whenever I have the money I buy a little meat or some eggs, and I put a few vegetables into the soup. But this 'Proteins are the building blocks of the body!' What crap! And I'd like to see that teacher bathe my family every day. She doesn't have to walk two blocks to the spigot and wait for half an hour to fill her buckets."

I told María exactly how to get to the clinic and when she should come. María assured me that she would be there and would bring her sister too.

Several months later I went to visit her. She lived in a barrio wedged between the slaughterhouse and a balsa wood factory. To get to her house I had to balance on a path of slippery logs across slimy green mud. Pigs and ducks mucked about in the puddles. Flies from the slaughterhouse buzzed thickly; vultures swooped down low. Children's eyes, large and dark in round faces, followed me curiously from every doorway.

I had to climb a ladder to get to the house. María served me strong sweet coffee and introduced me to her eight children. I asked her how she had liked the clinic. "Well, I haven't been yet. My first month I had to take Pancho to the hospital because he had a terrible case of *la gripe*, and I had to go back two times before they saw us. Then the next month I didn't go because my sister didn't feel well, and she had no money for the bus. And now I'm pregnant so I'll wait till after the baby before I go." She didn't seem remotely upset by the prospect of the ninth mouth to feed. She had accepted her fate—it was God's will.

I went to see the new baby shortly after her birth. María was cradling a tiny bundle against her breast. From the tightly wrapped swaddling blanket peered a little face with large black eyes, a beaked nose, and, already, little gold earrings. In that small dark room where María had so few possessions, the baby was a treasure.

One Saturday Paul and I went with José, a young hard-working doctor from the clinic, out to a rice-growing town called Babahoyo. We were to meet with a group of doctors who wanted to start a family planning program. When we got to the hospital, they were waiting for the nurse to bring in a patient to be fitted with an intrauterine device. Another Peace Corps volunteer had gone to find some women she knew were interested in having one, but the doctors grew impatient. They led us to a large operating room with screenless windows overlooking the river and the lawn where goats grazed. A wasp buzzed around us.

Finally a nurse led in a small woman wearing a white hospital robe. When she saw the men, the woman moaned and clutched her robe tightly. The doctor told her to lie down on the table. While José demonstrated the proper method for inserting the loop, some doctors watched with interest and the others stood smoking and laughing by the window. When José finished, the head doctor said, "Very interesting. Now why don't you take it out?"

"Take it out!" José said, shocked. "Doesn't she want it?"

"How should I know?" shrugged the doctor. "She's just a patient we brought in for the demonstration."

One of the doctors later began to offer birth control to his patients. He took the loops, which he got for free, broke them in half, then charged the patients for inserting them. He made a good profit on a useless, dangerous piece of goods.

FAMILY PLANNING OR POPULATION CONTROL?

For me the clinic was a place to work that provided a structure for my days, a set of tasks to accomplish, and some good friends. I had quickly lost hope of "converting the masses" and had resigned myself to helping a few women get some information that they might or might not use.

But for the Peace Corps staff, the clinic was an outpost on the front lines of the battle against underdevelopment. Along with most other North Americans working in Ecuador, they thought that Ecuador would never develop until its birth rate was reduced. How could the government provide adequate schools, housing, food, and jobs for its population when it was growing at a rate of 3 percent a year?

Working in the clinic, I was participating directly in a U.S. aid program. Wymberley Coerr, the U.S. ambassador to Ecuador, had outlined his goals for that aid program to our group shortly after we had arrived in Ecuador. Our task as volunteers, he said, would be like the chore of Sisyphus. We would slowly roll the rock of progress up the mountain, only to have it come crashing down on us and our projects. He went on to say:

> All representatives of the American government here, 300 Peace Corps Volunteers, 180 employees of the Agency for International Development, 60 members of the State Department, 40 workers at the NASA Observatory, and 87 military personnel must have the same purpose. That purpose is to help Ecuador maintain its independence. Some of the private American money that is at work in this country is for humanitarian purposes, but most of the aid given Ecuador is justified by our country's interests.
>
> The problem here, of course, is the lack of technical and economic development. But we have to work with the power structure that exists, and there is not much we can do about inequality there.

By "helping Ecuador maintain its independence," the ambassador meant keeping the Communists or Socialists from gaining power in Ecuador. The aid he was talking about was allotted according to categories. Most of the money came not as grants but as loans, about half of which went to the military for new weapons and training soldiers in counterinsurgency techniques for putting down revolutionary movements. The rest was distributed by the Agency for International Development (AID) to projects like police training, agricultural experimentation, vocational high schools, universities, highways, and birth control clinics.

AID maintained a large office in Quito. The important posts were held by North Americans, with Ecuadorian consultants and secretaries and chauffeurs. Most of the money lent or granted to Ecuador was spent to pay the salaries of North American technicians, to buy machinery and equipment from the United States, and to ship it on North American vessels. AID subsidizes many U.S. export firms.

The head of AID's Population Office was an ex-haberdasher from New Mexico, who had obtained his job through some political connections back home. When I went to ask him for money to print up some educational pamphlets he answered, "Oh yes, Raquel, you've got a good idea. Giving them birth control without explaining it to them is like giving the niggers at home the vote without teaching them how to use it." Outraged by his remark, I complained to his superiors. He was incompetent as well, and a few months later he was transferred back to Washington.

As time went on I came to disagree more and more with the premises of the birth control program. It is inhumane for the United States to grant money only to support clinics for preventing Ecuadorian women from having babies while ignoring clinics that would insure that babies already born would lead healthy lives. I heard many Peace Corps and AID officials say that Ecuador should pass a law that women be sterilized after their second baby. Officials do not hesitate to interfere with the lives of poor women, but they do nothing about interfering with an unjust economic system that prevents the poor from enjoying a decent standard of living no matter how few children they had.

In any country where women have no job opportunities and where their entire childhood prepares them to be mothers, they are not voluntarily going to have small families. Population growth has slowed down only in countries where women have incentives to work, to fulfill themselves in ways other than motherhood.

LA OLIGARQUIA

None of the aid programs was designed to shift any significant amount of wealth or power from the ruling class to the poor. *La oligarquía* runs Ecuador. It is the relatively small group of families who own the banks, the large haciendas, the factories, the export-import companies, and the newspapers. Its sons lead the military and govern the Church. The children go to private school, then to college in the States. They come back and marry within their own circle. They can buy whatever luxuries and power they desire.

When the daughter of Guayaquil's major banana exporter got married, her father imported the food from Texas and flew in a chef from Paris. He lavished tens of thousands of dollars to feed and entertain the other members of Guayaquil's high society. The couple honeymooned in Miami, then returned to a mansion staffed with a cook, a gardener, several maids, and a laundress.

The only oligarch we ever visited was Galo Plaza Lasso, a former president of Ecuador, a respected United Nations truce negotiator, and the current head of the Organization of American States. He is reputed to be the nation's most progressive landlord.

A friend of Paul's brother knew him well, so when Geoff came to visit us, we called Galo Plaza up. He invited us to visit him at his hacienda. We drove through the high Andean valley north from Quito. Green fields formed neat patchwork up the slopes of the mountains, and white houses clustered cozily in villages gathered around the church plaza. The volcanic peak of Mount Chimborazo loomed ahead of us, majestically capped with snow. Puffy white clouds dotted the deep

93

blue sky. After the heat and dust of the coast, it was like driving through a cool, crisp heaven.

Galo Plaza's mansion was surrounded by beautiful lawns and gardens. When we drove up, his wife and daughter were just setting off on horseback. In their long cloaks they looked like medieval ladies. They told us to get "the boy over there" to show us the field where the master was overseeing the wheat harvest.

The "boy" was a middle-aged Indian. He guided us to a hilly meadow where two enormous mowing machines were cutting and raking great swathes of wheat. Dozens of people stooped behind, picking up whatever stalks the machines had missed. They too were Indians. Each man wore a long braid down his back, a woven wool poncho, and a felt brimmed hat; each woman had on an embroidered blouse, a long wool skirt, a poncho, and a hat. Don Galo Plaza was leaning against his Mercedes, carefully watching the work. Except for the modern machines and car, it was a scene from feudal times. We waded through waist-high wheat to reach him and shook hands.

At first he talked in great detail about the skillful way he had won a truce in the Middle East and on Cyprus. Then he told us about his haciendas, and the enlightened way in which he manages them.

"I am very good to my Indians, much better than my neighbors are. They resent me because I pay my workers more than they want to. They say I give their Indians wrong ideas. But I believe in helping them. I've built them a school and hired a teacher. The more years of schooling they have, the more I pay them. I've even arranged for the very bright ones to get scholarships to the American School in Quito. One of our boys is a doctor now, and his brother is a concert musician. I've also told the priest that he cannot preach against birth control.

"I told the Peace Corps that I would provide a house if they would send me two volunteers to work with the women on marketing their handcrafts. They do the most lovely embroidery —you've probably seen the costumes that the waitresses in the Hotel Quito wear. Well, we make them here.

"The one thing I refuse to give them is money for their fiestas. I hate to see them waste their hard-earned sucres on liquor. So many Indians around here are drunk, but not mine. They are very happy working for me."

After leaving the hacienda, we drove through a neighboring village. We passed several Indians walking home from town. The men leaned drunkenly on their wives. When they saw our car full of white people, the men mechanically raised their hands to doff their hats. One man, though, bent to pick up a rock. His wife knocked it from his hand.

Remembering Galo Plaza's smugness, I got angry. Perhaps he was a generous *patrón* (boss), but he still retained all the power. He decided what and how much to give "his" Indians. Although he was a well-known politician, we never heard him speak out publicly against the discrimination and exploitation practiced against the Indians by the whites.

Many Indian communities have no schools. Many Indians live on corn and potatoes. Many can't vote because they speak no Spanish. Their problems will not be solved by a nice patrón like Galo Plaza. They need the opportunity to work, to learn, and to earn. They need to be allowed to live in dignity. Nobody in the government represents them.

The oligarchy was not about to relinquish its powers voluntarily. Whenever students demonstrated, workers went on strike, or people marched to protest the rising cost of food, the government called out the police or army to disperse the troublesome crowd. We saw countless demonstrations coming down the main street and always ducked into stores to escape from the inevitable tear gas (supplied by U.S. aid), which met every march.

AID's programs weren't designed to change the social structure, as Amabassador Coerr had explicitly stated. The U.S. policy stemmed from the assumption that it was better to accept the status quo than to risk change. Moreover, the U.S. State Department and U.S. businessmen operating in Guayaquil saw the status quo as beneficial to U.S. interests.

The Ecuadorian government allowed importers like Standard Fruit to buy up the banana harvest at low prices; it allowed Grace Lines to do most of the shipping between the United States and Ecuador and to pay low taxes on their business investments; it granted generous terms to Texaco to encourage exploration for oil in the Amazon basin. With the energy crisis, it is important to Texaco and to the way the U.S. economy currently runs to get that oil as cheaply as possible. Ecuador is not only a source of raw materials for our consumption, but it buys millions of dollars' worth of goods produced in the States. Politically, the United States wants Ecuador to continue to support our foreign policy moves, both in the United Nations and the Organization of American States.

For these reasons and more, our State Department wants to keep a conservative government in power in Ecuador.

It became increasingly clear to us through our experiences in the barrios, city hall, and the AID offices that the poverty and injustice which characterized Ecuadorian society could only be ended by some drastically different government. We had no real idea of what kind. We had heard that Communism had brought some big changes to Cuba, but we didn't know much about them. I had never studied any system of government except our own. I had never studied economics; Socialism was a dirty word in Wellesley. I knew there was more to a Communist system than dictatorship, but I had no idea of what one might be like in Ecuador. It was obvious that Ecuador was neither Communist nor Socialist. Neither was it a democracy.

It was an oligarchy: a government of the rich, by the rich, and for the rich.

PILAR

Sometimes we became totally absorbed in Guayaquil. We were unofficially adopted by the Olmedos, a middle-class family who welcomed us to their house for meals, parties, hot showers, and evenings of conversation. They lived in a neighborhood of neatly paved roads, walled yards, flowering vines, red-tiled roofs, and large stucco houses.

Señora Olmedo, or Mamá, was a widow with ten children whose chief goal was to marry off her daughters. Her great joy in life came from her grandchildren, and her favorite pastime was gossiping. She liked us because we talked with her and because she hoped that one of our Peace Corps friends would take an interest in one of her daughters. She was delighted when Paul and her beautiful daughter Carmen (who worked for the phone company and had a photographic memory) decided to share a birthday party. We cooked platters of *arroz con pollo* (chicken with rice), baked cakes, and bought beer and sodas. The Olmedo living room was crowded, and we danced until three in the morning.

Pilar Olmedo became one of my closest friends. She was one of the first women to graduate from the School of Architecture at the University of Guayaquil. She worked at the Seguro Social (the Social Security office), designing houses. Her job was intellectually challenging, but it depressed her to design homes for middle-class people when the poor needed decent housing so desperately. She longed for work that would be consistent with her political values.

The culture's machismo had wounded her. The other architects didn't take her ideas seriously. Because she was still single, they were always proposing an affair with her. She was very attractive, very smart, and very witty. She didn't want a husband unless he would share her work and her ideas, unless he would respect her individuality as well as admire her beauty. She was afraid of the marriages she saw imprisoning her older sister and many of her friends.

We often talked about these problems. I shared with her some of the tensions that Paul and I felt with each other, and told her how we dealt with them. She wanted to change her society, I wanted to change mine. She was searching for answers, and so was I. It was a relief to have a friend with whom I had so much in common and with whom I could enjoy so many pleasant activities in Guayaquil, like trips to the beach and nights at the movies.

YANQUI GO HOME

Our satisfaction with new friends and our increasing enjoyment of life in Guayaquil did not mitigate our increasing dissatisfaction with the Peace Corps organization and its staff members.

At first we tried to argue with the directors about poor planning, which had brought us to a city where we had so little useful work to do. We discovered that the Peace Corps had drawn up a five-year plan for its projects but had excluded Ecuadorians from the planning. When we tried to persuade them to reevaluate their projects to include the people whom they were supposed to help, the director insisted that he knew better than they did what was best for Ecuador.

We wanted the Peace Corps staff to help our group focus on a satisfying work project or to declare our program a failure and pay our way home. The director was an authoritarian man who did not like to be challenged. The man who replaced our first director in Guayaquil was vague, inexperienced, and drank too much. For more than a year we argued with our chiefs, exchanging recriminations. Sometimes the other volunteers agreed with us; other times they thought we were overintellectual malcontents. One couple told us that they would be satisfied with their accomplishments if all they did was show some Ecuadorians that there were North Americans who liked rice. Others stayed at home or played cards, criticizing the ignorant "Ekkies" to each other. Others worked very hard on projects but felt the results were insignificant. Many agreed with our arguments but didn't want to cause trouble. They were avoiding the draft, or they didn't want to leave yet. Some volunteers found their work both satisfying and rewarding.

We had some very close friends too. About a year after we got to Ecuador, we joined with three other volunteers in writing a letter to the *New York Times* protesting the war in Vietnam. Our director threatened us with expulsion, but the Peace Corps staff in Washington decided that it would hurt the Peace Corps image if they kicked out volunteers for expressing political opinions back home.

Later eight of us wrote and signed an article calling for the internationalization of the Peace Corps. We felt that volunteers would be more useful if they came from different cultures, representing the United Nations rather than the United States. Our article began, "We joined the Peace Corps because we thought it would afford us a means of helping nations without imposing the United States' cultural and political values on them. We were wrong. We now see the Peace Corps is as arrogant and colonialist as the government of which it is part." The article was published in eight newspapers in the States.

Our angry frustration with the Peace Corps, both its motives and objectives, crystallized and took on momentum, so that when we found ourselves in the Bogotá cafeteria bombarded with shouts of "Yanqui go home!" we were already seriously considering the idea.

After the incident Paul wrote an article for the *Village Voice* called "Yanqui Go Home, and Maybe We Should." He criticized the Peace Corps in particular, and U.S. policies in general. Our local director (a third man, for the second one had been sent home when too many volunteers complained about his irresponsibility and drinking) told us to pack our bags. Hoffman, the country director, was coming down from Quito, and he would surely tell us to go home.

When Hoffman walked into the Peace Corps office, we were prepared for a scene. Instead he smiled nervously and said, "I have good news for you. The Peace Corps has finally decided to classify the Guayaquil Urban Community Development Project a failure. You're free to go home whenever you like, and we'll pay the way. Paul and Rachel, wouldn't you like to be home for Thanksgiving?"

We told him that the course we were teaching in community development wouldn't be over until December 1. We would leave in mid-December. Four other volunteers decided to leave at the same time.

Our last few weeks were full of sad and happy moments. We were ecstatic to discover that I was pregnant. We were touched when our class presented us with an elaborate diploma at the graduation ceremony. It hangs now in our kitchen. Pilar organized a good-by party, and her house was crowded with people we had come to love. Now that we were about to leave, Guayaquil felt secure, like home. The United States was the scary new place. I clung to each moment, dreading the hour of departure.

Julio and Evangelina and their boys, Pilar and her family, Jorge Rodríguez, and many of our students came to the airport. We hugged them all. As the jet took off Paul and I held hands tightly, and I started to sob. It was December of 1967.

5

New York Again

STEAK AND ICE CREAM

Sudden new images hit us immediately back in New York. In Guayaquil it had been the stench of rotting fruit and urine, the clinging heat, the beggars, the tattered shacks, the hovering vultures. Here it was food. Everywhere in those pre-Christmas days after our return I saw food. People in restaurants, cafes, coffee shops, bars, and pizza parlors hurriedly lifting forks, chewing, swallowing, raising glasses, wiping chins. Their plates were loaded with thick steaks, hamburgers, French fries, salads, ice cream sundaes, pies, and cakes.

The supermarkets looked enormous; their aisles stretched back and back, loaded with bright cans, mountains of fruit, slabs of meat. Everything elaborately packaged. Life in New York seemed to consist of rushing from one meal to the next, the journey punctuated by stops in wonderland department stores and stints in elegantly furnished glass offices.

Paul's sister Holly took me shopping to buy some winter clothes. I'd lost so much weight from hepatitis, parasites, and tropical heat that none of my old clothes fit. At the top of the escalator in Lord and Taylor's we saw a mannequin clad in a rainbow dress of shining sequins.

Holly urged me to try on the dress. It was the most sensational, glittering piece of clothing I'd ever put on. It was the embodiment of Christmas in New York. And I bought it! It cost me ninety dollars, Julio's entire salary for four months. I've worn it every Christmas since—still loving it and hating it.

We fell in love with the United States again. We were glad to be away from its overseas representatives and back with people who cared about ideas, who talked about books, who were idealistic. It was nourishing to be with our families and close friends. The country had changed enormously while we were away—mini-skirts and pant-suits, long hair, angry loud rock music, and huge, militant antiwar demonstrations—but it was our country. We belonged here; we were no longer outsiders.

BITTER SPRING

Or were we? As our new freedoms became familiar and the thrill of hot showers and good ice cream wore off we found that our minds began to drift away from conversations. Our memories held us subtly apart from our friends. How were we to lead our lives in this affluent country, knowing that the Martínezes in colonia Emiliano Zapata and our friends in the barrios of Guayaquil were living on the edge of starvation?

What had begun as a passionate love affair with our country slipped into a more complicated love-hate relationship. One minute I'd be walking down the street thinking happily about the baby kicking around inside of me. Then I'd notice a trash can spilling junk over onto the sidewalk and flash with fury. How the tienda keeper in our barrio would have coveted those empty bottles!

Paul and I moved to Washington to resume our lives as part of "radical America." He had a grant to write a book about his earlier experiences in the civil rights movement and the Peace Corps. He called his book *The Making of an Un-American*. I was working with a group of returned volunteers trying to communicate the urgency of our experiences to an indifferent public caught up in the pursuit of their livelihoods and in the turmoil of domestic politics.

Martin Luther King, Jr., then Robert Kennedy were assassinated. Their deaths saddened and enraged us all. They made us question more deeply and pessimistically where our country was headed.

Pilar came to visit us that bitter spring in 1968. She liked our friends and the energy with which we were trying to take on the issues of foreign policy and domestic injustice. She was still pessimistic about changing Ecuador and very discouraged about her chances of getting ahead in her profession. She had applied for a scholarship to study city planning in Spain.

When she got back home she wrote us, "Before I came to the States I thought our problems were much bigger than yours, but now I feel glad to be Ecuadorian because our country seems manageable. I am hopeful that we can somehow change, but your country is too big, too strong, and too violent to save itself."

I knew what she meant, although I didn't completely agree. The job of changing both countries was enormous. The spring had reminded me of how deep racism is in our country and how strong the military influence is in foreign policy. In Ecuador I had seen clearly what an underdeveloped country is and had witnessed the failure of the free enterprise system to do anything about it. What I still wanted to understand was some alternative to the present conditions.

CUBA?

Some of the returned volunteers I was working with had been in Peru, Panama, Chile, and Honduras. Their experiences in the Peace Corps had been similar to ours. The social and political structures of the countries where they worked were also like Ecuador's. They too were angry at our government's support of those oligarchies.

Gradually we all became interested in Cuba. Its new government was becoming a legend among people critical of our foreign policy. It was a little David who had kicked the Yankee Goliath and survived. A friend of ours returned from a visit there with glowing descriptions of new schools, a teacher training institute, and pioneering day care centers. He marveled at the people's revolutionary consciousness. He told us that we could probably get a visa, for the Cubans welcomed journalists who would be open-minded about their Socialist approach to development. Paul and I were interested.

We decided to wait until the baby was born. It would be awkward to travel through a hot country on bumpy roads in the late months of pregnancy. I imagined that bathrooms would be far between.

Washington was getting unbearably hot and muggy as the summer drew near, and we decided to stay with Paul's parents on Martha's Vineyard. He could write there, and I'd have the baby. We hurried through our natural childbirth classes.

From the way many people reacted to the idea of giving birth on Martha's Vineyard, you'd have thought we were going back into the Peace Corps. When Paul pointed out to a friend of his mother's that women have babies at home in most parts of the world and survive, she nodded. "Oh yes, you're used to primitive things, aren't you?" It was hard for middle-class Americans to imagine life's most natural event taking place outside a large, well-equipped metropolitan hospital.

The Martha's Vineyard Hospital was small but perfectly modern and nicely intimate. The doctor had never delivered a baby without first anesthetizing the mother; the hospital had never permitted a father to be present in the delivery room. But the doctor was interested in our plan and persuaded the director to change hospital policy. We were his first natural childbirth delivery.

The labor was long, but I got through it with Paul's help. He counted the lengths of my contractions, coached me on the special breathing, fed me ice chips for my thirst, and held my hand. He urged me not to give in to the pain. Only once, very near the end, I begged for anesthesia. The doctor calmly persuaded me that the worst was over. Finally, just on the stroke of midnight I pushed as hard as I could. My whole body shuddered with the effort. Then all at once, Lisa was out! When the doctor laid her wet body on my stomach, Paul and I were crying and shouting with joy. It was one of the happiest, proudest moments of our lives.

The doctor was also impressed by the delivery. He saw how lively and alert Lisa was, and how joyous Paul and I were. After that, he urged other parents to try it too and made it general hospital practice to allow fathers into the delivery room. Unintentionally we had done on Martha's Vineyard what we never did in the Peace Corps. We introduced a new concept into a community.

When Lisa was a year old we decided it was time to go to Cuba. At that point we began the most complicated part of our trip—dealing with the State Department. Its policy was to deny permission to U.S. citizens to travel to Cuba, except for professional journalists, or academics. I had not written enough then to establish myself as a professional. My sister Connie was coming with us, and she had none of those credentials either.

The practical consequence of being denied permission was

that the Mexican government refused to give us a visa to return from Cuba via Mexico. Mexico was the only country in the Western Hemisphere from which commercial planes flew to Havana. Our travel route would be New York to Mexico City to Havana to Madrid to New York. The airport officials in Mexico City took our photographs, stamped our passports "*Salió para Cuba*" (Departed to Cuba) in huge letters, and filled out forms in triplicate. I'm sure that those forms ended up in our files in the FBI and the CIA.

6

Visiting Cuba

A DIFFERENT SET OF BLINDERS

When I went to Ecuador I wore a set of blinders—I was going to help those poor people—which took a long time to lose. Going to Cuba I wore a different set—I wanted to see a Revolution which had solved all those problems I knew about in Mexico, Ecuador, and Colombia and other parts of Latin America. I wanted hope.

In Cuba I found it. Cuba excited me and moved me. Tears welled in my eyes when I saw each new project that was teaching, feeding, or healing children. I compared everything I saw to Mexico and Ecuador, to Cambridge and Chicago. I thought of Socorro's makeshift medical treatment, Rolandito's crowded bamboo shack, of Mrs. Smith keeping her daughter home from school because she couldn't afford new shoes, and Mrs. Jackson traveling forty miles to shop because the stores in Cambridge wouldn't hire black clerks. I visited a maternity hospital in Cuba and found myself unable to explain to some new mothers why I had had to pay $1,000 for Lisa's birth. Their deliveries had cost them nothing.

My blinders, though, interfered with my learning, just as they had in Ecuador. I was so eager to be impressed that I didn't push to find out what lay below the dazzling surface I saw. I was afraid that the Cubans, whose intelligence, experience, and accomplishments I admired so much, would think me unbearably bourgeois if I asked critical questions or argued. I minimized disturbing incidents or critical opinions simply because I did not wish to see my dream-come-true vanish.

Even though I know that a tourist misses much of the truth, I still chose to travel widely, to see a lot in less depth. I didn't ask to live in one place so I could learn more about fewer people. Therefore, I didn't have the same kinds of long friendships that I had in Mexico and Ecuador, which provided enough trust for frank discussions. I don't know how it feels to experience the Cuban government's pervasive, demanding presence in so many areas of one's daily life. Nevertheless, what I saw seems to be confirmed by Cuba's growing prosperity, independence, and acceptance by other Latin American countries. And I can describe the experiences which made me so enthusiastic about Socialism in Cuba.

HAVANA LIBRE

When our plane landed at José Martí Airport in Havana, we were met by Felipe, a handsome young black man from the Cuban Institute for Friendship with the People (a government agency known by its Spanish acronym ICAP). While Felipe got our visas stamped, our shoes sprayed against hoof-and-mouth disease, and our bags through customs, we sat in the waiting room drinking daiquiris. The Cuban men's and women's volleyball teams, returning victorious from an inter-American match in Mexico City, had come in on the same plane. They were drinking daiquiris too, standing with their friends and families, laughing, hugging, and exchanging presents.

As we rode into the city in a red 1959 Cadillac, Felipe pointed out some of the sights. We passed a huge billboard proclaiming ¡*Vietnam Vencerá*! (Vietnam Will Win!) in giant letters. The night air was hot and heavy—tropical like Guayaquil's, but more fragrant. The streets were wide and spotless and almost barren of cars. The buildings were modern; their windows were decorated with signs and posters—not merchandise. In *La Rampa*, the modern entertainment district, the streets were filled with people. A long line waited outside a movie theater that advertised *Seven Brides for Seven Brothers*, an old film from the United States. Another group of people waited to get into a hotel nightclub. An even longer line snaked through a grassy park. Felipe told us that people waited for three hours to get into Copelia's, an airily designed new ice cream parlor that served forty flavors.

Felipe registered us in the Havana Libre Hotel and took us up to our rooms. Then he hurried off to spend the remaining few hours of the evening with his family. He promised to meet us the next day.

The Havana Libre had been part of the Hilton chain before it had been nationalized by the Cuban revolutionary government. Its architecture and furnishings were of the familiar international style that seems to emanate Muzak from every wall. In the old days it had swarmed with North American tourists on their gambling, sun-seeking vacations. Now the hotel houses foreign visitors and technical consultants of all nationalities. The furnishings are clean but worn.

As soon as Felipe left, we changed our clothes and put Lisa into her blue canvas backpack. Paul lifted her onto his shoulders, and we set out into Havana's Saturday night.

The sight of little Lisa perched in her backpack delighted the people crowding the streets. Small boys called out "¡*Coche, coche*!" ("Car, car!") and actually rolled on the sidewalk with laughter. Many assumed we were Russians, and called out to us, "¡*Ola tovarishchi*!" ("Hello comrades!") Women reached out to pat Lisa or to ask us where the pack came from. When they found out that we were from the States they were excited and curious. "How did you get here? Won't your government punish you?" "How do you like Cuba?" "Is it the custom in your country for the men to carry babies like that?" "Who will win the World Series?" It felt wonderful not to hear any of the flattering, wheedling, or hostile remarks that we'd grown to expect as gringos in other parts of Latin America.

On the Malecón, the famous avenue bordering the harbor, we met two teen-aged Cuban couples, dressed up for an evening of dancing. Hearing our English, they stopped us to talk. "Are you Americans?" One of the boys invited us to his house, and promised us some whisky. They wanted to know all about the United States. The boys were desperate to go there. They wanted to get out of Cuba—it was too drab, the stores were empty, they couldn't buy records, fancy clothes, or any of the other things they longed for. They had to work too hard. The girls shared many of their complaints, but they didn't want to leave their families.

We politely declined the invitation to visit. "Nice talking with you anyway," said the tallest one. "Say hello to Ringo Starr for us." They walked up toward the night club. Were they typical Cuban teen-agers?

Within an hour we'd had two conflicting impressions—the friendly, cheerful crowds, and the disenchanted teen-agers. I was exhausted but impatient to see more. I was relieved of my usual worry that I wouldn't be able to get along with people or to enjoy myself. Until that night I hadn't been sure.

I had always despised the hysterical anti-Communism espoused by so many people in the United States. The House Un-American Activities Committee, inspired by Joseph McCarthy, had persecuted the parents of some of my friends back

in the early 1950s. The right of an individual to join the political party of her preference was as important a principle of
my childhood as the Girl Scout motto. Yet when it came time
to visit a Communist country, I couldn't believe that Communists
would actually be people like me. What would they laugh
about? What would they talk about? What would I have in
common with them? It was obvious that in spite of my intellectual resistance to anti-Communism I had unconsciously absorbed the emotional attitudes prevalent in the United States.
I felt like kicking myself for being so foolish.

TOURING CUBA

Felipe had explained that Cuba did not have enough gasoline,
cars, buses, hotels, and restaurants to allow people to travel
randomly. The government had to plan their tours so it could
ration the gas and reserve hotel rooms so that guests would find
bed and food wherever they went. Felipe arranged an itinerary
so we could be sure of having appointments to tour factories,
schools, or hospitals in each town we came to. He assigned us
a guide, Tulio, to make sure we had no problems.

I still wondered whether traveling with a guide would keep
us from getting a true impression of Cuba. But it turned out
that Tulio would usually rest in his room when we came to a
new place, leaving us to wander around by ourselves for a few
hours. People were often curious, sometimes suspicious, about
who we were and what we were doing. Some showed us around,
introduced us to their families, and talked enthusiastically about
all the changes that had taken place in their town. Others turned
away. Occasionally people asked how much our clothing had
cost and inquired tentatively about buying a shirt or pair of
sunglasses. On the whole island I saw only one beggar. I took

pictures everywhere, and was stopped only twice from photo-graphing something—once the entrance to a military base and once the new machinery that some British engineers were in-stalling in a fertilizer factory.

DAY CARE

Lisa spent four of her six weeks in Cuba in the Heroic Vietnam Day Care Center in Havana; three of those weeks she stayed day and night while we were off on a trip. It wasn't easy for me to leave her in an unfamiliar place, but it seemed better for her and me than to drag her on tours of schools and factories where she had to stay quiet and got no nap. Friends had assured us that the centers were clean and that the *asistentes*, or at-tendants, paid close, loving attention to the children.

Lisa liked the center immediately. When I picked her up the first afternoon, she looked at me with a smug look as if to say that she had her own place now. The asistente who brought her down to us that day grew fond of her. She bathed her twice a day, dusted her liberally with powder, and combed her hair in a dainty new style.

All the toddlers stayed upstairs in two large sunny rooms. Each had his own crib, but they ate together in high chairs around a table, sat on potties in a row, and played together in large playpens for short periods each day. Their routine in-cluded two naps, lunch, two baths, and two snacks.

The center occupied an elegant mansion that had once be-longed to a wealthy family that had fled Cuba shortly after the Revolution. Their extra cars had been expropriated, their large landholdings transformed into an agricultural collective, and their business nationalized. Their way of life was dead. The rooms that had once seen balls and sumptuous dinner parties now housed 100 children while their parents worked.

If I had had to leave Lisa in that center five days a week from infancy, I would have had some reservations about it. The asistentes valued cleanliness and order more than free play that might result in messiness. Some of the toys were kept on the shelves unless visitors were touring the center. The day's program was so structured, and the variety of toys was so limited, that I would worry that she would not have the opportunity to develop her own identity and explore her special abilities.

On the other hand, I would never worry about her safety or her health; I would never be nervous about a baby-sitter. She would learn to relate to other children and to take the group's needs into consideration. I'd be able to work without spending a large part of my earnings on day care. (At home, day care costs me forty dollars a week, and I devote an enormous amount of time and energy to our small parents' cooperative center. I love its program, but I believe that all parents are entitled to free day care for their children.)

A REVOLUTIONARY COMPAÑERA

Lisa needed a complete medical check-up before she was permitted to start at the center. We took her to a clinic where she had an examination, various tests, and a TB shot—all for free. It would have cost us at least fifty dollars at home.

While waiting for her, I suddenly felt faint. En route to Cuba, I had picked up a stomach virus in Mexico. I was also in the early stages of a new pregnancy and was suffering from morning sickness. Feeling dizzy, I put my head between my knees. A nurse rushed over. She sent me upstairs and called for a doctor. Within five minutes I was lying on a clean bed with a needle in my arm, being fed intravenously.

A middle-aged woman was on the bed next to me, also hooked up to a jar of glucose. She was due for major surgery the next day, but was receiving this dose to give her the strength to attend her son's wedding that afternoon. She was delighted to have a captive audience. Telling me about the Revolution, she became so excited that the nurse had to come in and make her lie down.

She had grown up in the country, she said, far from Havana. Her parents had been sugar workers on a United Fruit Company plantation. She grew up to work in the plantation office. Her husband found work there too, after he had fled from Franco's Spain. Together, they had tried unsuccessfully to organize the workers into a union. She said she had always dreamed of the day the workers would get decent pay and could send their children to school, but she had never imagined that day would come in her lifetime.

The changes she had seen in Cuba since the Revolution thrilled her. Her children loved their jobs. Her daughter taught economics at the University in Havana, her oldest son was a technician in the sugar ministry, and her "baby," the bridegroom, was an army major. After retiring, she and her husband moved to Havana to be near the children. He assists the manager of the local government-run grocery store. She spends her free time working for the neighborhood organization called the Committee for the Defense of the Revolution, the CDR.

The CDRs were formed right after the Revolution, she explained, to watch out for sabotage and other counterrevolutionary activities. In those days, the wealthy Cubans who had backed Batista, Cuba's deposed, corrupt, and brutal dictator, were trying to overthrow Castro's government. The committee members rotated on watch duty to report anything suspicious.

Now, she went on, there was little counterrevolutionary activity, so the CDR members served as liaisons between the city government and the neighborhoods. They canvassed houses, urging mothers to take their children for their injections, send them to school regularly, and donate blood when necessary. They organized groups of volunteers to work in the fields on

Sundays, planting coffee bushes or harvesting citrus fruits to help supply Havana with food. They kept a watch for people who appeared to be staying home from work for no obvious reason, and they talked to families whose behavior they thought was antisocial. Their other job was to take inventories of the household goods of people who had applied to leave Cuba. The emigrés were allowed only their most personal portable possessions. Their houses, furniture, and cars became the property of the government.

I asked whether she would report someone who listened to the Radio Free Cuba programs that the U.S. government beams into Cuba over Voice of America radio. "Heavens no!" she said. "In fact we think it's good for people to hear the lies the Yanquis are telling about us. But I would be suspicious if somebody was always huddled over his radio or if people went in and out of his house frequently. You know that they've caught spies broadcasting messages out of Havana!"

I wondered what the border was between necessary vigilance and excessive interference in individual lives. Where did community service end and invasion of privacy begin? How free were people to be themselves? I could only know that by living there for a while.

The time passed quickly in that spotless little room. I liked the woman's cheerful friendliness and her enthusiasm. Her husband came in and sat with us. He told us some jokes and asked me questions about the United States. Like most Cubans we met, he wanted to know what the North American people thought about Cuba. He assumed that the people's attitude in my country would be different from the government's. He was worried, too, that my government would punish me when I got back home. All too soon the nurse came in to release us from the plastic tubes. Neither of us had to pay for our treatments.

THE REVOLUTION

Cuba is the one country in this hemisphere that exists completely apart from United States influence, although it is of course affected by the U.S. economic boycott.

Before the Revolution, Cuba was almost a part of the United States. At one time, proslavery lobbies in the Congress had pushed to annex it. Then in 1898, the U.S. Army, led by Teddy Roosevelt's Rough Riders, intervened in the Cuban War for Independence from Spain, and easily defeated the Spanish forces, whose weapons were old-fashioned and whose strength had been sapped by years of fighting Cuban guerrillas. The United States took Puerto Rico and the Philippines as spoils of victory, but granted Cuba its independence—with some restrictions. Our government retained the right to establish a naval base at Guantánamo (which we still operate) and to intervene in Cuba whenever events took the "wrong" turn. On several occasions, when North American business interests were threatened, the Marines went into Cuba. The U.S. ambassador was always involved when Cuban presidents were overthrown.

Cuba's beauty, its climate, its beaches, and the warm energy of its people made it a popular resort with North Americans. Millions of tourists spent their vacations swimming, dining, and gambling. Some owned large homes there. U.S. corporations invested millions of dollars in sugar plantations, oil refineries, railroads, communications systems, and hotels. They owned the Cuban economy. They built a modern infrastructure of highways, ports, office buildings, and railroads. For the wealthy, Havana was an exciting city. The Mafia also found it a good place from which to operate, since the government was so corruptible. Narcotics, prostitution, and gambling became lucrative businesses there.

Life for the Cubans who didn't belong to the elite was not so good. The vast majority of Cubans lived in violent, crowded, filthy slums, or in thatched cottages in the countryside. Their children were hungry and uneducated. They could find seasonal jobs at best. For the poor, there were few opportunities to get ahead.

In the 1950s, General Fulgencio Batista's dictatorship, which the United States had long supported, became intolerable. Cubans of all classes joined into a loose coalition to overthrow him. Fidel Castro led a small but growing and effective army of guerrilla fighters in the mountains. Other revolutionaries organized strikes in the cities and cooperated with the sabotage in the factories and cane fields. Urban liberals raised funds for the rebels. In 1958 Castro's troops forced the Cuban army, which had bombed villages with napalm supplied by the United States, to surrender. Batista fled. At the head of an enormous victory procession, Castro and his soldiers marched across Cuba to Havana.

Once Castro had taken power, he and his fellow revolutionaries discovered that driving out Batista was only the beginning of a long battle to end poverty, injustice, and underdevelopment. They finally decided that they would have to build an entirely new system of government based on new ideas. Their first priority was to give the government control of Cuba's natural resources and industries. That meant nationalizing the Standard Oil refinery, the United Fruit plantations, the railroad, the telegraph and telephone companies, the factories, and the hotels.

These nationalizations enraged the U. S. ambassador, the corporations, and the State Department. The United States stopped buying Cuban sugar, and forbade U.S. companies from doing business with Cuba. Any ship that docked in Cuba was forbidden to dock at a U.S. port. The State Department pressured all the countries of Latin America to exclude Cuba from the Organization of American States and to break off diplomatic and trade relations. Only Mexico resisted. As a result, the Cubans had only a few European countries and the Soviet Union as a market for sugar and as a supplier of machinery. They couldn't replace any worn-out parts on the U.S. machinery they already had. That's why we made our tour in a 1959 Cadillac. The Cubans hadn't any newer models.

In the spring of 1960, a CIA-funded army of Cuban emigrés invaded Cuba at the Bay of Pigs. Faulty CIA intelligence had led the emigrés to believe that the Cuban people would rise up in support. Instead the Cubans crushed the invaders. Rather than executing the captives, Castro agreed to send them back to the United States in exchange for medicines and tractors. Ever since then, the CIA has continued to infiltrate Cuba with saboteurs, spies, and would-be assassins.

THE BATTLE AGAINST
UNDERDEVELOPMENT

Almost every program that we had thought AID should have been promoting in Ecuador or that the War on Poverty should have included in the United States was under way in Cuba—and much more. Thousands of new schools had been built in the cities and towns and out in the countryside. Mansions had been converted into day care centers or boarding schools for high school students who lived far away.

Hospitals and clinics stood where none had ever been. Medical school graduates, half of whom were women, were required to spend two years working in rural clinics and hospitals. Pledged not to go into private practice, they had agreed to accept salaries no higher than those of other health workers. Massive public health campaigns had eliminated malaria and polio. The death rate from gastroenteritis, the disease which had almost killed Socorro and which claimed so many young lives in Guayaquil, had declined drastically. We saw that graphically when we visited a children's hospital ward. Where the beds had once been filled with dehydrated children, we found only three in the huge room. The hospital gave their mothers free meals and trained them to care for their children in the ward. They also showed them drops of water under a microscope, so they could see the germs that were making their children so ill. From then on, they would certainly boil their water and be able to explain to their neighbors why it was important to do so.

One of Castro's first priorities had been to convert the mental hospital—whose horrendous conditions had been the focus of prerevolutionary student demonstrations—into a modern, airy, spacious facility without bars. The patients were treated with drugs and occupational, vocational, and recreational therapies instead of lock and key. We saw patients working in rose gardens, caring for thousands of chickens, which they ship into Havana's grocery stores every two months, and building furniture for day care centers. They knew that their work was contributing to their society.

New crops, like pineapples and high-yield, extra nutritious rice, were being harvested; new lands were being tilled, planted, and fertilized. The F-1 cow, a cross between the hardy Zebu and championship Holstein bulls, was giving eight times the milk her mother did. Yogurt had become a staple of the Cuban diet.

Gradually people were being moved out of their thatched *bohíos* and decaying tenements into rent-free prefabricated cement houses or housing projects. Using local materials and traditions, young architects were designing sophisticated new hotels, where workers could spend their two-week vacations. Engineers were building roads to connect small towns once linked to the outside world by mud trails.

A massive campaign by volunteer teachers had lowered the illiteracy rate from 26 percent to 3 percent. Classroom teachers, often too young and inexperienced because the rapidly expanding number of pupils exceeded the supply of trained teachers, were supplemented by educational TV. Cuban athletes provided formidable competition in the Pan-American games and in the Olympics. Some of the most exciting posters and the most creative films in the world began to come out of Cuba.

We visited a town on Cuba's northern coast that seemed to exemplify many of these changes. Nuevitas used to be a sleepy port whose sole economic support came from the ships that loaded sugar at its docks. The Nuevitans had worked as stevedores, bartenders, waiters, prostitutes, and gamblers; or they didn't work at all.

After the Revolution, Che Guevara visited Nuevitas. As the man in charge of devising an industrial development plan for the country, he decided that Nuevitas was a good site for an electrical generating plant, a cement and a fertilizer factory, and a deep-water port. Less than ten years later Fidel dedicated the giant fertilizer plant. The thermoelectric station is now generating power for the province, and the port is larger than the one at Guayaquil.

Building up Nuevitas was not easy. The town is hot and lies several hours from the nearest city—not a location to attract new workers. At first they would stay only long enough to save money and then leave to join their families. The government planners soon saw they would have to make the town more attractive so that families would want to stay there. The government built new apartment buildings, sports fields, restaurants, a theater, and a day care center, and planted trees to screen the industrial section off from the residential area. They built schools for children and for workers. Where there used to be but one doctor there are now thirty-five. The one tiny hospital was replaced by a large one and several outlying clinics. The town has become a small city, and the factories have all been completed ahead of schedule.

LA ZAFRA

Most of the Cubans we met spoke enthusiastically about the Revolution, about Castro, and about their commitment to keeping up the rugged pace of work. Their attitude was strikingly different from the Ecuadorians'. Cab drivers in Guayaquil helplessly bemoaned the potholes in the road and the vendors in the streets; our neighbors warned us that all Ecuadorians were pickpockets, just out for themselves and not to be trusted; some students even told us they wished the United States would come in to set up an honest government. They blamed the corrupt state of their politics on the Spanish conquerors; if the Anglo-Saxons had arrived first, they thought, things would have been different.

A typical Cuban comment, however, was, "Well, it's true that we've come a long way, but we must continue working hard if we're ever to beat underdevelopment. We've had to sacrifice, but we share the sacrifices, and they will pay off soon. Don't tell your friends back home that we have solved all our problems, because we still have much to do."

Ordinary people, not just government bureaucrats, made those remarks, many times. One old cab driver added, when I told him I'd learned my Spanish in Ecuador, "Oh, it's terrible how those people are starving. We in Cuba can't stop working until they are as free as we are. We will have to grow even more food than our people need."

One person would eagerly tell us about the time she had seen Fidel, another would quote from a speech of Castro's, another would laughingly repeat one of his jokes. He seemed to have been everywhere and talked with everyone on the island. People boasted of how much he knew about cattle-breeding or teased him for being a bad sport at basketball—apparently he hates to admit defeat, so prolongs the game until he wins.

At the time we were in Cuba, the country was mobilizing itself for a national campaign to harvest 10 million tons of sugar. Almost everyone took a month off from his regular job to cut cane or to work on enlarging the refineries. Offices closed down or ran with skeleton staffs. Retired people operated the elevators in our hotel so the young ones could go to the fields. Trucks and trains were diverted to carrying cane-cutters or the cut cane.

The latest harvest totals were reported like the results of the World Series. Everyone was looking forward to July 26, when they would celebrate the end of the *zafra*, or harvest. The government was stockpiling beer and rum for the holiday. At a vacation resort high in the Sierra Maestra, a couple had invited us to their cottage for beer and crackers. In a chatty tone, the hostess remarked, "The ten million tons are on the way, you know!" as she passed the crackers.

There was something even more impressive about the Revolution than the buildings, the energy, and the enthusiasm. We noticed time and again how the Revolution had given so many people the opportunity to realize more of their own individual potential. They were doing jobs that they had never imagined they were capable of ten years earlier.

THREE CUBAN PORTRAITS

We visited a milk factory the government had nationalized. I couldn't evaluate the technical performance of the factory (which had been owned by the Nestlé Corporation), since I know nothing about the process of canning and evaporating milk. But I did talk with one of the factory's workers, Mario. His job was to develop new milk products. He had originated the production of dried malted milk and had developed a new baby cereal.

Mario remembered spending mornings as a boy waiting with his father outside the Nestlé factory gate, hoping that someone would be sick so his father could earn a day's wages. There were no other factories in town, and wages were low because there were so many more workers than jobs. Nobody could organize a union when hundreds of men, desperate to feed their families, would scab.

The factory produced enough milk to supply the families that could afford it. During the dry season, when cows give less milk, workers were laid off. At the same time, hundreds of thousands of families couldn't afford milk. Pregnant women, nursing mothers, and small children often went without it.

Hoping to find a job, Mario went to Havana. After the Revolution, he came back and went to work at the plant. Castro had promised that the government would provide a quart of milk a day for every child under seven and for every pregnant woman and nursing mother. The factory increased its production eight-fold, but milk still had to be rationed to make sure that the people who needed it most got their daily supply.

Starting as a machine operator, Mario was later sent to school to study food, nutrition, and dairy science. He had recently represented Cuba at a World Health Organization conference in Chile and was proud that the Cubans were doing more than any other Latin American country to improve the diet of their people. He told me how the factory was planning to expand its production. He felt satisfied, he said, working to provide milk for Cuban children rather than to increase the profits of the Nestlé Corporation.

Miguel, the driver of the red Cadillac which took people from all nations to see the works of the revolutionary government, had a similar story. Before the Revolution he had been a chauffeur for a wealthy family that paid him six dollars a week. As the family's maid, his wife earned the same wages. Miguel and his wife are black, and in prerevolutionary Cuba they could not find better jobs. They expected that their children would have had the same problems in that racist society.

"I never talked politics with my boss," Miguel told us. "He was frightened of the guerrillas, and he hoped that Fidel would be shot. I never told him that I was with Fidel. Then one day, soon after Fidel came to Havana, I went to work and found nobody was there. The whole family had gone to Miami. They must have taken millions of dollars with them. My wife and I were so glad. We didn't like being servants."

Miguel had learned to play excellent chess from some Russian passengers, but preferred to travel with the North Vietnamese, as they would not eat a bite unless their driver was at the table with them. His Cadillac was old, but he knew every part of it. He is the boss of his car. He had learned to patch anything, since he couldn't get any replacement parts. During our trip we had three flat tires, and we once had to wait a day for a new tire to be flown from Havana.

Miguel's wife manages the neighborhood grocery store. Their daughter was planning to become a doctor, their son an army officer. One afternoon as we drove past some kids walking home from school, Paul heard Miguel say softly to himself, "Our youth, what a treasure!" I wondered how many adults in the States would look at a bunch of school kids as a boon.

At a hotel in Santiago we met a family of sugar workers on their vacation. Their ten-month-old son, Eliazer, was one of the handsomest babies I had ever seen. His large, dark eyes reflected what seemed to be an extraordinary wisdom. His mother told me what it had been like to grow up as a black on a sugar plantation owned by North Americans.

"When I was small, my father was a cane-cutter. He could work only three or four months a year. They paid him almost nothing for breaking his back out in their fields. What he did earn they took back at the company store. Each year we ended up owing them more than we did the year before.

"We lived in a little shack far away from the big house where the manager lived. He didn't want any black people living near his family. The white workers had their section, and we had ours—the littlest houses on the worst land. The white workers had their social club, but we had none. When the zafra was over, we lived off the little garden behind our house and on the rice and beans we bought on credit. I went to school whenever I wasn't working, but I never learned how to read.

"Now I go to night classes. I've learned to read and to do office work. Most days I stay extra hours because we've got so much to do. We're doubling the size of the mill to help with the ten million tons. Eliazer goes to his day care center, but sometimes I bring him into the office. He's so smart, he knows what a typewriter does. His daddy takes him out with him too. When my husband is not harvesting, he's fertilizing or planting new fields or digging irrigation ditches. The only trouble now is that we have no time to rest.

"You know," she said, "my grandfather who is seventy-two came into this office one day and said to me, 'Caridad, whatever happens, you have to protect this Revolution with your life. It has given you everything you have.'"

During our trip I often tried to imagine that Pilar was with us and could see what the Cubans were doing. We met an architecture student who had just come back from three months of field work with her class, more than half of whom were women. They had been designing a vacation resort for workers and spent the weekends planting pineapples. They were just about to set off for a month of cutting sugar cane. The previous year, the class project had been to plan a playground in Havana, and the following year they would help a community group plan its new housing.

I was curious, too, how Pilar would get along with the university students. As far as we could tell, they supported their government enthusiastically, a far cry from the perpetually striking students at the University of Guayaquil. Would Pilar have wanted more critical debate at the university?

I wrote her a lengthy letter. "Here I don't think you would feel as isolated as you do in Guayaquil. Your work would be part of a national effort, a contribution to society—not just a way to earn a living. In Cuba, there is so much work to be done that there aren't enough people to do it. In Ecuador and in the United States, there is just as much to be done, but our governments are not committed to doing it. The private companies won't do it either, since they won't make a profit from it. So the work doesn't get done and the people don't have jobs. The main thing you would take back from Cuba is a vision of what your country could be like, and a new hope that it can change."

The plane from Havana to Madrid—crammed with Cuban water polo players, families leaving Cuba for self-imposed exile, and foreign visitors—flew up into the orange sunset. We circled back over the island, lying dark dusky green in the gleaming sea. Waves broke on white, palm-fringed beaches. People will never believe what I tell them about Cuba, I thought. It sounds too good.

WHAT DOES FREEDOM MEAN?

I was partly right. Although some North Americans were only interested in Cuba's successes, most judged the country against standards that were higher than their expectations for any non-Socialist country. To satisfy them, not only must the Cubans end poverty, hunger, and ration lines, but they must also abolish all vestiges of racism and machismo. Furthermore, they must achieve this massive social change while maintaining the same level of civil liberties as we enjoy in the United States. With typical North American arrogance, these critics consider Cuban Socialism a failure because it has not achieved all the goals *they* have set for it.

Nevertheless, I too came back with some reservations about what we had seen in Cuba. We had a couple of experiences which contradicted the favorable impressions we gathered: we met more people like those teen-agers on the Malecón. At the time, in 1969, the negative images seemed minor compared to the positive ones. Later, I wondered whether they were symptoms of larger problems we didn't grasp or were just kinks in a system that had not yet fully developed.

Now, in 1975, I realize that I can't evaluate those impressions without going back to Cuba. I describe them because they were part of our experience, but my present impression, based on TV shows, news articles, and conversations with friends who have been there more recently, is that consumer shortages and excessive security measures are not such a problem. The rise in the price of sugar has greatly increased Cuba's income, and the government has imported many more consumer goods. The government is now trying to develop a system for electing local officials, and was pleased with the people's participation in the elections in the province of Matanzas.

In the spring of 1975 Castro presented the draft of a new constitution to the Cubans. After thorough discussions have taken place, everyone over sixteen will vote whether to approve it. The constitution is designed to decentralize the government by providing for the election of provincial assemblies and a national assembly of some four hundred representatives. The national assembly will select a thirty-one-member state council to run the government. The head of the council will also be the head of state.

Among other provisions, the constitution also proposes that housework be shared equally between women and men.

One afternoon we wandered through an old town across the

bay from Havana. It was a port through which sailors had traditionally smuggled contraband, and it was still the center of several cults that had grown out of the religion brought to Cuba by African slaves. An old woman invited us in to visit, and we were listening to her explain how to make medicinal teas from the various plants growing in her yard. Maybe we had been asking too many questions around town, maybe some zealous CDR member became suspicious of the strangers. Anyway, a little man in sneakers came into the yard and asked us to follow him. We had to wait for three hours in the police station while the officials checked our identities. They were courteous, and they apologized profusely for the inconvenience. Nevertheless, we had been detained for doing nothing. We couldn't tell if the incident was a typical case of the police detaining people who aroused the suspicions of a neighbor or a fluke because we were foreigners in a community still vulnerable to smugglers.

The government, and many of the Cuban people, believe that their revolution is under the constant threat of attack from Cuban exiles supported by the CIA. They worry about sabotage and possible attempts to assassinate Castro. They have captured spies who give validity to their fears. They remember the 1960 Bay of Pigs invasion and the 1962 Missile Crisis. They know that the U.S. government has isolated Cuba and done its best to weaken it.

I understood the need for vigilance, for security, and even for the CDR nightwatches. I could see that the government feared that too much dissent, encouraged and fomented by enemy agents, could weaken their efforts and jeopardize their goals. Cuba's history, after all, is one of successive autocratic rulers—not popular democrats. Very few Cubans have ever enjoyed the freedom to do just what they wanted.

Nevertheless, as events in the United States and the Soviet Union have shown, concern with national security can easily be turned into concern with self-serving political security, and an autocratic ruler can use the mechanism of the police and the army to eliminate legitimate, constructive dissent if he perceives it as a threat to his personal power.

The Cuban Revolution, like the American, produced many refugees. Those teen-agers on the Malecón were not the only people we met who didn't like living in Cuba. On another afternoon, two black teen-aged girls approached Paul. In lowered voices they asked if there was any way he could help them get to the United States. They said they were desperate to go some place where they could walk into any restaurant and order what they wanted. He asked them if they realized how many poor people there were in the States and how many black people faced special difficulties in finding jobs and decent housing. They didn't care. To them freedom meant the opportunity to spend your money on whatever you wanted, not on what the government chose to make available. Even though they knew they might be poor, they didn't quite believe it. They wanted the freedom to dream of things they might buy one day.

Their discontent with Cuba's lack of consumer goods—radios, TVs, clothes, snacks, toys—is the result of both the U.S. economic boycott and the Cuban government's deliberate decision to put every possible dollar into machinery, agricultural tools, fertilizers, and seeds in order to lay the base for future economic growth. Cuba annually spends about 30 percent of its budget on projects for future development, a much higher rate than for any other country in this hemisphere. That decision means, though, that the Cubans do not spend the money they earn from exporting sugar, cigars, rum, meats, and fruits on importing luxury consumer goods. It means that Cuban goods are rationed, so everybody buys the same amount of food and clothing, and nobody buys too much. It also means that the Cuban people don't eat the best meat, fish, and fruits that they raise, for those are exported to earn more income.

The Ecuadorian government is different. It does not prevent wealthy Ecuadorians from sending their money to foreign banks or from spending their money on imported luxuries. As a result, only a small amount of the money earned in Ecuador is invested in projects for future growth. Individuals and private companies send their profits abroad, where they earn more. The government taxes little, so has only small sums to spend on public projects like schools, hospitals, roads, and factories.

The Cuban government must obviously remain sensitive to public opinion; it must judge when it may relax its austerity so that the people won't become completely demoralized. When we were there, because the people had complained, Castro had just rescinded a decision to close the nightclubs in Havana, which he thought were vestiges of capitalist decadence. Communication between the people and their government is structured through the Communist party, which has chapters in every place of work and in every neighborhood. Delegates are elected by the people they work or live with. It was impossible to tell how the structure worked from our short visit, but our impression was that communication came more often from the top down than from the bottom up, though the process worked both ways at times.

This centralization of decision-making may sometimes be detrimental to the implementation of the goals the government decides on. If dissent is stifled at the local level, then local problems may arise which could have been foreseen and prevented. For example, thousands of hours went into planting coffee bushes that died because soil conditions weren't right. Generally, workers are encouraged to discuss the directives that come down from the Central Committee of the Communist Party, which is the major decision-making body in Cuba—they have a say in how to implement them but not in whether they are based on the best policy.

The new draft of the constitution was written to overcome

these problems by creating the mechanisms for more localized control and more worker participation in decision-making.

LUCIA

I met Lucia while visiting the Karl Marx High School in Havana. She came over to talk when she saw my camera. "Was it easy to get one in the United States?" she asked wistfully.

She was an introspective teen-ager. She was feeling depressed that day because her father had just left for exile in Spain. He had been a successful merchant who had stayed to work for the government economics ministry after the Revolution. Finally, he felt overwhelmed by the bureaucracy; he couldn't stand working in an office. He missed being able to build his own business, to take his own risks, and to enjoy the rewards of his personal success. He was an individualist in a collective society. The tensions in him destroyed his marriage. When he decided to leave, his wife divorced him. Torn between parents she loved, Lucia chose to stay with her mother and with the Revolution.

She was studying math at a high school that was geared to academically talented students. Lucia expected to become an economist or a mathematician after graduating from the university. She was proud of the Revolution's accomplishments, and she felt it was her duty to contribute her talents to her country.

Although she knew she was good at math, she really wanted to be a writer and photographer, but she couldn't buy a camera— there were none for sale. And she didn't want to write for *Granma*, the official newspaper, which reported only the government's view of domestic and world politics. Lucia wanted to write long essays about everyday, human things that were going on in Cuba, based on her own experience and perceptions.

She told me that she would stay in Cuba and work as hard as she could for the Revolution. The day might come, though, she added, when she would decide that she had to start writing about ideas the government might not like. Then she would have to make a difficult decision. Would she stay or go?

In many ways, Lucia was like me. I imagined myself in her position, asking the same question, feeling the same conflicts. I'm not sure what I would do if I were a Cuban, but I do know I'd be proud of what the Revolution had accomplished.

7

Latin America on My Mind

JUAREZ REVISITED

In the summer of 1973 Paul and I went back to visit the Martínezes. The streets of Juárez looked more crowded and shabby than ever. The beggars were scattered through the market crowds. Sick, crippled, young and old, they sought us out to plead for a little charity.

We remembered the route to the bus stop and climbed on the familiar orange bus. The driver had to tell us where to get off though, because there were so many new buildings along the main road that we didn't recognize the corner.

Paula was just coming down the street as we got off. We hugged each other, then stepped back to look. She appeared almost exactly the same to us, but she said we were fatter, which was true. Proudly she showed us how the children had grown. Ernesto, who was born after we left for Ecuador, was a husky seven-year-old with two missing front teeth. Pepe impressed us immediately. He'd become a competent, resourceful young man, old for his twelve years, who goes to high school and helps his father make simple carved wooden frames for the Day-Glo paintings downtown merchants sell to tourists.

Paula and Mingo were strict with Pepe. Now that he was so big and smart, they worried. Juárez is a city of hustlers, of people who offer schemes to get rich quickly but illegally. It's also the departure point for Mexicans who hope to make a living in the States. Pepe's intelligence, his street-smarts, and his ambitions may make it intolerable for him to settle for his father's way of life. School already bores him. He has no money for college, no conventional way of entering the middle class. He may possibly find good work in Juárez, but more likely he will decide to leave his home, just as his parents did before him. Paula was worried that he would get into trouble and lived with the fear that he would leave home.

Maela was eighteen. She rose at five each morning to reach her new job at an RCA plant, where she assembles TV parts. Although she is glad for the money which helps the family so, she feels exploited. She knows that thirty dollars a week is low pay for forty hours of work. Anybody doing the same job in the States would get at least three times that much. She has used her earnings to buy twin beds for the girls' new room and covered them with matching spreads. All four girls have chosen pictures of their favorite singers and TV stars to decorate the walls of their room.

Socorro, a beautiful girl with the same saucy smile as ever, plans to work in the factory when she gets old enough, but now she stays home. She earns a little money cutting and setting hair for the neighbors, but mostly she hangs out with her friends talking about boys or flirting with them. She had embroidered her bluejeans with peace signs. She dropped out of school because she thought it was too hard and boring.

Beneath Mingo's shy, unassuming manner was a new pride and self-confidence. He had made a success of his carpentry— in the summer tourist season he had more orders for frames than he and Pepe could handle. He'd hired two nephews and his brother-in-law to help him. He'd spent his earnings on improvements for the home. He had enlarged the kitchen, added on the girls' room, built a work shed with a wood stove, and made a bath and washtub in the backyard. His brother-in-law and family sleep in one of the carpentry sheds in the backyard. He bought a second-hand TV, an ancient water-cooled fan, and new chairs for the living room. They also own a car—a battered green and white Ford, which they drive only through the colonias because nobody has a driver's license.

Paula was more relaxed too, and the wrinkle between her brows was not so deep. "This house is a palace for us, Raquel. Who would ever have thought we would have four rooms?" Quickly she added, though, so as not to tempt fate, "It could all vanish. We're not rich. We still just eat beans and tortillas. Prices have gone up so we can't afford anything more."

We walked through the colonia one evening with Pepe and Socorro. More houses than ever grew out of its terraced hillsides; the colonias lapped up the slopes of the mountains. Children ran in the dirt streets, playing catch or tag, laughing and shouting. Radios sent their music dancing softly through the air. Dogs barked, roosters crowed a last good night. A man passed us on his donkey cart, empty at the end of a long day except for a few melons bouncing in the back. Families in old cars jolted over the rutted road. An old man called out to advertise the hot corn he was selling from a steaming tub. The children mimicked his sad, tired cry. Inside the lighted door of a tienda some women laughed. Socorro went in to buy us all Chiclets.

Towering above the hilltop, a thick white cloud turned a slow orange-red with the setting sun. Far below, across the Rio Grande, the lights of the El Paso Natural Gas Company shone tall amid a sea of brightly sprawled suburbs.

We left our Juárez family sadly. Who knew when we would see each other again?

135

AND ECUADOR

Beneath the Amazonian jungle in Ecuador lie vast, newly discovered oil fields. A multimillion-dollar pipe line has been built over the Andes by U.S. oil companies to take the precious liquid out to waiting tankers. Ecuador is on the brink of becoming a wealthy nation. But the people of Guayaquil's barrios know only that a sudden inflation has driven up the price of rice, sugar, and everything else. None of the new oil revenues has reached the barrios, although luxurious new office buildings and condominiums have given downtown Guayaquil a more prosperous, cosmopolitan look.

Paul and I haven't been able to go back to Guayaquil, but some friends have visited Julio and Evangelina. We also get frequent letters. Julio lost his job when the German company left Guayaquil. With borrowed money he bought a small cart, which he loads with green bananas and pushes through the streets, peddling his wares. He also bought a pair of pigs whose offspring he sells. "Julio is always tired," Evangelina writes. She ended her last letter: "We are really sad for the events now happening in town. On August 10 a teacher got shot in a public demonstration, and ever since there has been uneasiness in town and the schools are closed. I ask God that these problems will be solved soon."

Despite these friendships, it is hard for us to keep the realities of Latin America sharply focused in our minds. Events here become more immediate, more important. The poverty there is so terrible that it is sometimes hard for me to believe that my memories are correct, not romantic exaggerations.

A COUP IN CHILE

In the fall of 1974, I was jolted out of my cloud of blurred memories when I learned that the Central Intelligence Agency had spent more than $8 million to overthrow the democratically elected Socialist government of Chile. Once again I was confronted urgently with the political truth we had learned in Ecuador: the United States government will not allow the people of Latin America to determine their own futures. Our government decides which group of oligarchs is acceptable and then enforces its choice with "foreign aid," airplanes, tanks, and soldiers. U.S. Marines have invaded various Latin American countries, the CIA has overthrown governments. In Ecuador, our intervention is subtly designed to keep the existing oligarchy in power.

In Chile, we blatantly undermined a government we did not like and then conspired to overthrow it. When the Chileans elected a Socialist, Salvador Allende, as their president in 1970, he promised to do many of the things that Castro had accomplished in Cuba. Chile had a long history of democracy—the longest in Latin America—and Allende swore to maintain its democratic institutions. He raised wages and the standard of living for the poor, so that many could buy meat for the first time in their lives. He distributed the lands from large haciendas among peasant cooperatives. But when he nationalized the large U.S. mining companies, Anaconda Copper and Kennecott, which had been making enormous profits from the sale of cheap Chilean copper for years, new forces came into motion.

The U.S. government joined with the Chilean upper class and many of its middle-class people in denouncing Allende's reforms. These Chileans were losing their privileges and being

137

forced to sacrifice some of their comforts and authority. The United States was losing a major source of inexpensive copper. Furthermore, the Chileans were setting an example that might spread to the rest of Latin America.

Having foreseen the results of a Socialist victory, the U.S. government had helped to finance Allende's electoral defeat six years earlier, and had given money to his opponent in 1970. It also bribed Chilean congressmen to refuse to ratify Allende's election but could not muster enough support to prevent his taking office. Once Allende was president, President Nixon and Secretary of State Kissinger decided on a policy of creating economic chaos in Chile at the same time as they built up the political and military opposition. The United States cut off economic aid but increased the flow of funds and weapons to the military. The United States also pressured banks to refuse loans and credits Allende needed to import more food and to purchase new machinery. The CIA funded striking workers, organized protests, and supported right-wing newspapers and radio stations.

The Nixon-Kissinger strategy succeeded. The economy ran into increasingly severe problems, which Allende could not solve without outside assistance. Housewives marched to protest food shortages. Truck owners refused to deliver goods, thus bringing the economy to a virtual halt. Finally in September 1973 a group of generals, called the *junta*, organized a coup to "restore law and order."

Allende was murdered, and thousands of Chileans who had supported him were hunted down and jailed in concentration camps. The police killed several thousand, tortured thousands more, and still keep many in jails and camps. No one can criticize the present government without fear of arrest. Prices have gone so high that millions of Chileans are now worse off than they were before Allende. The ruling military junta has disbanded most of Allende's social programs.

In acknowledging the CIA role in Chile, President Ford stated that we had acted to "protect democracy, in the best interests of the people of the United States and of Chile." Yet no State Department official has publicly criticized the junta's blatant violations of international codes of human rights. The United States intervened because it did not want to see a Socialist government succeed in Latin America. Cuba was bad enough; our statesmen would not allow another left-wing government to take power and expropriate large companies, threaten the easy availability of raw materials, and support the foreign policy of the Soviet Union or the radical Third World nations. Even though the coup was carried out by Chileans and was based on widespread local dissatisfaction with Allende, the United States bears responsibility for its success.

A recently published book by an ex-CIA agent who worked in Ecuador during the early 1960s reveals that the CIA spent over half a million dollars a year to maintain its Ecuadorian and U.S. agents in their program of disrupting opposition political movements, reporting on the activities of Czech and Cuban diplomats, and disrupting student elections. If that money had been spent on clinics or schools, the Ecuadorians might be a little better off.

At this writing I feel almost the same urgency to do something about U.S. policy toward Latin America as when we got back from the Peace Corps. Our citizens have to elect a Congress and a president who will change the aim of our foreign policies. First we must stop sending troops and CIA agents to Latin America. We must cut off military aid to right-wing dictatorships and increase economic aid to governments that are pledged to use it for programs that will serve all the people, not just the oligarchs. Nations want to own and control their own natural resources, to be able to sell them at their own prices, and keep the revenues—just as we do. We can no longer monopolize them.

Throughout Latin America millions of people's lives are brutalized by poverty and tyranny. Slowly, but inexorably, movements will grow to change a system that allows the rich to live in luxury while the poor starve. We need a foreign policy that encourages the self-determination of those people, just as the French once helped the thirteen colonies in our struggle for self-determination. Socialist, Communist, and progressive nationalist governments are the only hope of the future for the majority of people who live in this hemisphere—our government must recognize that fact and cooperate with them. In helping to perpetuate unjust policies we are only prolonging misery no matter what our government's rhetoric would lead us to believe.

It will take time for the people of the United States to understand the needs of other peoples and to accept change. The world is small, its resources are finite. The most important thing I learned in Latin America is that our "national interest" is a selfish, outdated concept. Ultimately, it is only "human interests" that matter.

Postscript

Paul and I and our two children now live on the Upper West Side of Manhattan. We've chosen this neighborhood because so many different kinds of people live in it. The many Puerto Ricans and other Spanish Americans make us feel as if we're still part of Latin America, and Lisa and Mamu are learning much more about the world than we ever knew. We also want them to be proud of their own heritage, so we have begun to celebrate Jewish holidays and to ask my grandmother about the history of my family in New England.

The Peace Corps taught us that there is little that North Americans can do personally to help South Americans. But we can work to change our government's priorities and policies.

Sometimes it has seemed discouragingly difficult to make changes here in this country. Despite all the ground gained by the civil rights movement, the women's movement, and the peace movement, most of the country's problems remain the same. My working for McGovern for president and Ramsey Clark for

New York senator didn't seem to accomplish much. But things *are* changing—slowly. We must change ourselves as men and women, struggle against our own racism, and understand more about the realities of people in other countries. We have to change our institutions too. That kind of work is interesting, it's important, and it will ultimately lead to good things.

Emerson wrote: "If there is any period one would desire to be born in, is it not the age of Revolution?" I agree, and I hope we'll all get on with making one, each in our own way.

A Chronological Table
of U.S.–Latin American Relations

My primary source for this chronology is the excellent book *The United States and Latin America* by Richard J. Walton, published by The Seabury Press of New York in 1972. Where I have quoted from it, the page number is indicated in parentheses.

1823
Monroe Doctrine promulgated: no European power was to establish colonies in the Western Hemisphere nor interfere in the internal affairs of goverments there. Intended to defend the newly independent republics of Latin America from European imperialism.

1824
John Quincy Adams tells Simón Bolívar, leader of independence forces in Latin America, not to help Cuba and Puerto Rico fight for independence from Spain.

1827
John Quincy Adams offers to buy Texas from Mexico for $1 million.

1829

Simón Bolívar observes: "The United States appear to be destined by Providence to plague America with misery in the name of Liberty." Andrew Jackson offers to buy Texas for $5 million.

1835

The Anglo settlers of Texas declare themselves an independent republic. The United States remains neutral but angry at settlers' defeat at the Alamo.

1845

Congress votes to annex Texas. President James Polk offers to buy California and New Mexico. His offer rejected by Mexico.

1846

President Polk sends troops into Mexican territory. Mexican army attacks them, and United States declares war on Mexico.

1847

Polk sends General Winfield Scott to attack Mexico City.

1848

Treaty of Guadalupe Hidalgo signed, ceding California and New Mexico to the United States for $15 million.

1895

Secretary of State Richard Olney issues a message to the British government defining the U.S. conception of the meaning of the Monroe Doctrine:

> A doctrine of American public law, well founded in principle and abundantly sanctioned by precedent, which entitles and requires the United States to treat as an injury to itself the forcible assumption by a European power of political control over an American state. . . .
>
> Today the United States is practically sovereign on this continent, and its fiat is law upon the subjects to which it confines its interposition. Why? It is not because of the pure friendship or good will felt for it. It is not simply by reason of its high character as a civilized state, nor because wisdom and justice and equity are the invariable characteristics of the dealings of the United States. It is because, in addition to all other grounds,

144

its infinite resources combined with its isolated position render it master of the situation and practically invulnerable as against any or all other powers. (Pp. 51–52.)

1896

Republican Party wins the presidency. Senator Albert J. Beveridge articulates the conception of Manifest Destiny:

> The trade of the world shall be ours. . . . We will cover the ocean with our merchant marine. We will build a navy to the measure of our greatness. . . . Our institutions will follow the flag on the wings of commerce. And American law, American order, American civilization, and the American flag will plant themselves on shores hitherto bloody and benighted, but by those agencies of God henceforth to be made beautiful and bright. (P. 56.)

1898

The battleship *Maine* sails to Havana to convince the Spanish governor of Cuba to grant the Cubans more autonomy. The *Maine* inexplicably explodes, killing 260 crewmen. Public pressure mounts to join the Cuban War for Independence. Admiral George Dewey sails to Manila and captures the Philippines. The Marines invade Cuba in June. Armistice is signed in August, leaving Cuba nominally independent, but making Puerto Rico and the Philippines U.S. colonies.

1901

Congress draws up the Platt Amendment, defining Cuba's "independent" status: the United States retains the right to intervene during any situation which threatens Cuba's "independence" or "the maintenance of a government adequate for the protection of life, property, and individual liberty." (Although the Cuban people did not accept the amendment, it served as the justification for future interventions by the U.S. Marines against strikes, opposition forces, and "troublemakers.")

1903

The government of Colombia refuses a $10 million offer for land for the proposed Panama Canal. Theodore Roosevelt sends a navy ship to support secessionists fighting to make the Colombian province of Panama independent. He signs a treaty with the new Panamanian government, acquiring the land for $10 million as well as the right to "act as if the United States were sovereign" in the Canal Zone, a ten-mile-wide strip, and the right to protect Panama's independence.

1904

At a celebration of Cuban independence, Elihu Root reads a statement from Theodore Roosevelt putting forth his corollary to the Monroe Doctrine:

> All that we desire is to see all neighboring countries stable, orderly, and prosperous. . . . If a nation shows that it knows how to act with decency in industrial and political matters, if it keeps order and pays its obligations, then it need fear no interference from the United States. Brutal wrongdoings, or an impotence which results in the general loosening of the ties of civilized society, may finally require intervention by some civilized nation, and in the Western Hemisphere the United States cannot ignore this duty; but it remains true that our interests and those of our southern neighbors are in reality identical. All that we ask is that they shall govern themselves well, and be prosperous and orderly. (P. 75.)

Roosevelt initiates the era of Dollar Diplomacy—a period of increased investment in Latin American countries by U.S. mining, oil, railroad, fruit, and coffee companies. This policy is based partly on a desire to spread the "American way of life" to societies that are poor and disorganized, but it also ensures that any U.S. investor is able to operate without political or economic restrictions.

Also, the United States begins to run the customs service in the Dominican Republic because that government owes so much money to foreign creditors.

1906

William Howard Taft, secretary of war, declares himself provisional governor of Cuba when its government collapses. His rule is backed by U.S. troops. President Theodore Roosevelt states:

> I am so angry with that infernal little Cuban Republic that I would like to wipe its people off the face of the earth. All that

we wanted from them was that they behave themselves and be prosperous and happy so that we wouldn't have to interfere. And now, lo and behold, they have started an utterly pointless and unjustifiable revolution, and got things in such a snarl that we have no alternative but to intervene. (P. 78.)

1912

President Taft sends the Marines into Nicaragua to support an unpopular government. Wall Street bankers take over Nicaragua's financial management. (The Marines remain for thirteen years, then return when more fighting follows their departure. They withdraw finally in 1933, leaving the government in the hands of the head of the National Guard, General Anastasio Somoza. His family retains dictatorial power today and brutally suppresses dissent. The family is extremely wealthy, while the majority of the people live in poverty.)

1914

President Wilson sends Marines into Mexico to force an apology for the arrest of a party of American sailors. (Wilson thinks he is intervening against General Victoriano Huerta, an unpopular dictator, but the reaction to the intervention turns public opinion against the United States and increases Mexican political turmoil.)

1915

President Wilson sends the United States Navy to Haiti to restore order after an angry crowd killed the president, General Sam. Despite armed opposition, the navy begins to run the government, including the customs service, in order to collect revenues owed to foreign creditors. (The navy remains for nineteen years and kills thousands of Haitians who protest the U.S. presence between 1919 and 1934). It builds roads and hospitals, and trains a police force, which becomes the basis for the power of François Duvalier, a brutal dictator who does nothing to end Haiti's widespread poverty. His son is now the Haitian leader.)

1916

President Wilson sends the Marines to occupy politically chaotic Santo Domingo. The U.S. Navy takes over the government of the Dominican Republic, running all departments. The U.S. calls the armed resisters "bandits" and fights against them. Begins program of public works. (Remains in power until 1924 when Dominicans elect own president. He is overthrown by head of U.S.-trained National Guard Rafael Leonidas Trujillo, who becomes one of the most tyrannical rulers in Latin American history.)

1932
Franklin D. Roosevelt states in his inaugural address that his administration will seek to be a "Good Neighbor" to the rest of the world.

1934
The United States voluntarily abolishes the Platt Amendment, giving up its self-proclaimed right to intervene in Cuba. However, the U.S. ambassador retains a vital role in Cuban politics.

1936
The United States signs an "Additional Protocol Relative to Non-Intervention" at a Pan-American Conference in Buenos Aires, which Franklin Roosevelt attends. The first article reads: "The High Contracting Parties declared inadmissible the intervention of any one of them, directly or indirectly, and for whatever reason, in the internal and external affairs of any other of the parties." (P. 104.) The Latin American countries have been urging the United States to sign such a statement for over forty years. The principle of nonintervention is later incorporated in the United Nations Charter and the Organization of American States.

1940
The United States signs a mutual defense pact with many Latin American nations, assuring that, if the United States entered World War II, they would enter the war on the side of the United States. Guaranteed U.S. protection if attacked, they allow the United States to establish bases in Brazil, Mexico, Cuba, Panama, and Ecuador. The United States begins to rely heavily on trade with Latin America to provide the materials needed to fight the war. U.S. investments increase substantially, as does the money flowing to the upper classes of these countries.

1947
The Treaty of Rio de Janeiro is signed—Latin and North Ameri-

can countries to settle disputes on their own and not take them to the United Nations unless they cannot be settled within the hemisphere. The United States does not yield to Latin American requests for aid similar to that given to Europe under the Marshall Plan.

1948

The Organization of American States is formed. The United States priority is to keep Communism from Latin America, while the Latin Americans want economic aid. U.S. interests prevail with a resolution, "Preservation and Defense of Democracy in America," which states, among other things, that "because of its anti-democratic nature and interventionist tendency, the political action of international communism or of any totalitarianism is incompatible with the concept of American freedom." (P. 118.) The United States provides the governments of Latin America with military equipment, training, and advisers. Millions of dollars go for military aid, none for economic.

1952

President Eisenhower awards the Legion of Merit to Colonel Marcos Pérez Jiménez, the corrupt dictator of Venezuela who welcomed U.S. oil companies, used his police to guarantee no strikes or demonstrations, allowed them generous tax benefits, and enabled himself and the oil companies to profit handsomely from the exploitation of Venezuelan oil.

Also, the United States gives aid to Victor Paz Estenssoro, who had led a revolutionary campaign against the Bolivian landlords and tin mine owners. This is the first instance of the United States giving economic aid to a country which had nationalized U.S. property.

1953

Jacobo Arbenz Guzmán, the democratically elected president of Guatemala, expropriates 234,000 acres of uncultivated land from the United Fruit Company, as part of a campaign for land redistribution in a country where 2 percent of the people own 70 percent of the land. He offers to pay the company the property's value as declared on their tax forms. The company demands over thirty times that amount. John Foster Dulles, the U.S. secretary of state, begins to use diplomatic pressure to back United Fruit's demands. He issues a White Paper calling Arbenz too sympathetic to Communism. He assigns the CIA to overthrow the Arbenz government.

1954

Dulles uses his influence to win passage of a resolution at the tenth Pan-American Conference that:

> The domination or control of the political institutions of any American state by the international communist movement extending to this hemisphere the political system of an extra-continental power, would constitute a threat to the sovereignty and political independence of the American States, endangering the peace of America, and would call for a meeting of consultation to consider the adoption of appropriate action in accordance with existing treaties." (P. 126.)

Justifying his actions by this resolution, he sends U.S. pilots to bomb Guatemala City, and CIA-trained Guatemalan exiles to attack the Guatemalan Army. Arbenz resigns, to be succeeded by Colonel Castillo Armas, the leader of the exiles and a right-wing dictator. (He was to be assassinated in 1957, and to this date, Guatemala is torn apart by bloody fighting between left- and right-wing guerrillas, and thousands are jailed for opposing the government.)

1958

Vice-President Nixon visits Latin America. He is met with large hostile demonstrations. In Caracas, Venezuela, he has to be rescued by the military from an angry crowd surrounding his car.

1959

Led by Fidel Castro, a guerrilla army expels Batista from Cuba. Hostilities begin to escalate between the United States and Cuba. The United States stops buying sugar from Cuba, leaving the Cubans to find new markets for 90 percent of their crop.

1960

The United States agrees to pledge $50 million to the Inter-American Development Bank to be lent for social and economic improvement projects. (The Latin Americans had long sought this kind of aid, but the United States does not pledge it until after the anti-Nixon riots and the Cuban Revolution.)

1961

A force of fifteen hundred Cuban exiles, trained and financed by the CIA, land on the beach at the Bay of Pigs in Cuba. President Kennedy takes responsibility for allowing the invasion to take place and accepts the blame for its failure. He does not apologize for having violated the resolution of nonintervention. In fact, he restates the sixties interpretation of the Monroe Doctrine:

> But let the record show that our restraint is not inexhaustible. Should it ever appear that the inter-American doctrine of non-interference merely conceals or excuses a policy of non-action—if the nations of this Hemisphere should fail to meet their commitments against Communist penetration—then I want it clearly understood that this government will not hesitate in meeting its primary obligations which are to the security of our nation." (P. 137.)

Congress passes a bill refusing aid to any country which gives assistance to Cuba.

1962

The United States pressures the Organization of American States to expel Cuba. Half the supporting votes come from right-wing dictatorships, and Haiti supports the motion only after the United States promises to restore aid to Duvalier's dictatorship. Kennedy also announces the Alliance for Progress, a joint development program for the Americas, with the United States supplying the funds and the technical assistance, and the Latin American governments committing themselves to implementing these programs. The Alianza makes Kennedy a hero to millions of impoverished Latin Americans, and leads to the construction of new housing, roads, and schools. Kennedy hopes to persuade the Latin American governments to make enough changes so that the people will not turn to Communism as a solution to their problems. To ensure this, he funds a training and supply program for the military and police from all Latin American countries in order to effectively counter guerrilla movements. (Presidents Johnson, Nixon, and Ford have continued this program, which had strengthened the power of military dictators in many countries.)

In October, he warns the Russians that if they deliver missiles already en route to Cuba, the United States will blockade the ships. The Soviet Union turns the ships around and agrees to remove the missiles already in Cuba if the United States pledges never to invade Cuba. Kennedy agrees and the world is rescued from possible nuclear holocaust.

1965

Left-wing faction in the Dominican Republic military organizes a coup against President Donald Reid Cabral. The right wing organizes a countercoup. Many people join in the fighting to support the left-wing faction, and civil war spreads through the city of Santo Domingo. The U.S. ambassador decides that a left-wing victory would bring a Communist government. The U.S. sends in four hundred Marines, nominally to protect U.S. lives, but eventually to ensure the victory of the right-wing faction. The United States consults the Organization of American States after the Marines have been sent in. President Johnson explains his action was taken because "a band of communist conspirators" had taken over a "democratic revolution." (Since the invasion, the United States has given twice as much aid to the Dominican Republic as to any other nation in Latin America, but President Joaquín Balaguer, who won a U.S.-supervised election, has not made any fundamental changes in the country's political or economic structure; widespread poverty still prevails.)

1967

The United States and Panama agree to revise the Panama Canal Treaty to provide for a U.S.–Panamanian canal authority, a larger share of the canal's revenue for Panama, and the integration of the Canal Zone into Panama. (As of February 1975 the new treaty has not been approved, since Congress does not wish to grant Panama any control over the canal. New sites are under consideration for a sea-level canal.)

1969

Richard Nixon tells the foreign ministers of Latin America that he cannot promise much aid. He increases military aid, but not economic. Secretary of Treasury John Connally remarks that "we can afford to get tough with Latin America because we don't have any friends there anyway."

1970

The State Department gives the U.S. ambassador to Chile the "green light to move in the name of President Nixon" as well as "maximum authority to do all possible—short of Dominican Republic type action—to keep Allende from taking power." Unable to prevent Allende from assuming the presidency democratically, the CIA then works steadily to promote dissension and economic chaos and to foster the overthrow of Allende, which is successfully accomplished by the Chilean military in September 1973.

1974

Henry Kissinger meets with Latin American delegates in Mexico City and promises to open a "new dialogue" with Latin America. Two U.S. Senators visit Cuba, and there are hints of a future thaw in U.S.-Cuban relations as the majority of Latin American nations choose to reestablish diplomatic and trade relations with Cuba.

Books for Further Reading

Most books about Latin America are too dry, technical, or abstract to finish. Others are full of stereotypes about the quaintness or uniqueness of the "simple peasants." The books listed below are different. They convey a sense of people and places. They have taught me and tantalized me. Readers will learn from them, and may then go on to learn more by consulting their bibliographies.

MEXICO

LEWIS, OSCAR. *A Death in the Sánchez Family*. New York: Random House, 1969.

Tape-recorded interviews with three impoverished Mexicans, of the children of Sánchez, presenting their differing accounts of their aunt's death, wake, and burial, demonstrating how hard it is for poor people to bury their dead.

LEWIS, OSCAR. *Five Families*. New York: New American Library, Mentor Books, 1959.

"An intimate and objective picture of daily life in five Mexican families, four of which are in the lower income group," writes Lewis. Based on hours of taped interviews and days spent living with each of the families.

LEWIS, OSCAR. *The Children of Sánchez*. New York: Random House, Vintage Books, 1961.

"My purpose is to give the reader an inside view of family life and of what it means to grow up in a one-room home in a slum tenement in the heart of a great Latin American city which is undergoing a process of rapid social and economic change," writes Lewis. He succeeds wonderfully.

Mural Painting of the Mexican Revolution 1921–1960. Fondo Editorial de la Plástica Mexicana. Mexico City: Banco Nacional de Comercio Exterior, S.A., 1960.

A large book full of color reproductions of Mexican murals, with text tracing the development of the art.

WOMACK, JOHN, JR. *Zapata and the Mexican Revolution*. New York: Knopf, 1969.

An excellent view of the Mexican Revolution and the peasant movement for agrarian reform conveyed through the details of the life of one of its leaders.

ECUADOR

COWAN, PAUL. *The Making of an Un-American*. New York: The Viking Press and Delta Books, 1970.

My husband's autobiography, including his experience in the civil rights movement and the Peace Corps. Covers many parts of our life in Guayaquil that I didn't write about and gives a different perspective on some that I did.

LINKE, LILO. *Ecuador*. New York: Oxford University Press, 1960.

A dry, dull book, but it is full of facts about Ecuadorian geography, history, and political structure.

THOMSEN, MORITZ. *Living Poor*. New York: Ballantine Books, 1971.

A personal account of another Peace Corps volunteer's attempts to get a small coastal village to accept a chicken cooperative. Reveals many details of life in rural Ecuador and many attitudes of North Americans working in Latin America.

CUBA

DUMONT, RENÉ. *Is Cuba Socialist?* New York: The Viking Press, 1974.
An intelligent, readable critique of the Revolution by a long time sympathizer, a French agronomist who documents the short-comings of the Cuban government as they have affected the development of Cuban agriculture.

IGLESIAS, JOSÉ. *In the Fist of the Revolution.* New York: Random House, Vintage Books, 1969.
A lively account of the author's three-month stay in a small Cuban village where he went to experience the effects of the Revolution.

LEINER, MARVIN. *Children Are the Revolution.* New York: The Viking Press, 1974.
A study of Cuban day care centers, which includes good descriptions, facts, interviews, and balanced conclusions.

LOCKWOOD, LEE. *Castro's Cuba, Cuba's Fidel: An American Journalist's Inside Look at Today's Cuba in Text and Pictures.* New York: Macmillan, 1967.
Superb photographs and a long, fascinating interview with Fidel Castro.

RECKORD, BARRY. *Does Fidel Eat More Than Your Father? Conversations in Cuba.* New York: Praeger, 1971.
A Jamaican journalist talks with hundreds of Cubans and creates a rich, sympathetic picture of Cuban society.

SUTHERLAND, ELIZABETH. *The Youngest Revolution: A Personal Report on Cuba.* Photographs by Leroy Lucas. New York: The Dial Press, 1969.
A sympathetic description of the Cuban Revolution, focusing particularly on the attempt to eliminate racism and discrimination against women.

HISTORY

PRESCOTT, WILLIAM. *History of the Conquest of Mexico and History of the Conquest of Peru.* New York: Random House, Modern Library, n.d.
An extremely long but almost always fascinating history of the

Spanish conquest of the Aztec and Incan empires. Based on original documents, it also gives a detailed description of those civilizations.

POLITICS

MACEOIN, GARY. *Revolution Next Door: Latin America in the 1970's.* New York: Holt, Rinehart, and Winston, 1971.

The author reports on the views of the people he talked with on a 20,000-mile tour through Latin America. He explains why they blame the United States for the ever worsening human condition on their continent.

PETRAS, JAMES, and MAURICE ZEITLIN, eds. *Latin America, Reform or Revolution: A Reader.* New York: Fawcett, 1968.

An often hard to read but comprehensive anthology, which includes essays on politics, sociology, and development economics by leading Latin American and North American thinkers.

WALTON, RICHARD J. *The United States and Latin America.* New York: Seabury Press, 1972.

A concise, factual, and excellent history of relations between the United States and Latin America, tracing the interventions by the U.S. military in various countries and the policies our government has adopted toward the region from the Monroe Doctrine to the Alliance for Progress.

MISCELLANEOUS

LAPPE, FRANCES MOORE. *Diet for a Small Planet.* New York: Ballantine Books, 1971.

A book about proteins, which shows that our meat-based diet wastes protein needed by people in the rest of the world and gives good recipes for protein-rich dishes that use no meat.

MELVILLE, THOMAS, and MARJORIE MELVILLE. *Whose Heaven, Whose Earth?* New York: Knopf, 1971.

An ex-priest and an ex-nun describe the experiences in Guatemala which led them to take sides with Guatemalan revolutionaries and caused their expulsion from the country and brought about their decision to leave their religious orders.

ART AND LITERATURE

CARPENTER, HORTENSE, and JANET BROF, eds. *Doors and Mirrors: Fiction and Poetry from Spanish America, 1920–1970*. New York: Grossman Publishers, 1972.

A taste of contemporary, nonpolitical Latin American prose and poetry.

DE CASTRO, JOSUÉ. *Of Men and Crabs*. New York: Vanguard Press, 1970.

A powerful novel about a boy living in a swamp community in Recife, Brazil, where men and crabs fight hunger all day and night.

DOCKSTADER, FREDERICK J. *Indian Art in South America: Pre-Columbian and Contemporary Arts and Crafts*. Greenwich, Conn.: New York Graphic Society, 1967.

Text and photographs showing the varied beauty of ancient and modern Indian pottery, weaving, baskets, masks, and jewelry and the functions these objects served.

GARCÍA MÁRQUEZ, GABRIEL. *One Hundred Years of Solitude*. Translated by Gregory Rabassa. New York: Harper & Row, 1970.

An incredible, wonderful, crazy, powerful novel about the generations of one family in Latin America.

NERUDA, PABLO. *Five Decades: Poems 1920–1970*. New York: Grove Press, n.d.

ABOUT THE AUTHOR

A free-lance writer and photographer, Rachel Cowan lives in New York City with her husband and two children. Her work has appeared in *The Village Voice* and *The New York Times*. She continues to be active in community affairs, and has helped organize a local day care center.